the authentic musician

the

authentic

musician

Discovering Your Purpose As An Artist

john haddix

Authentic Artist Resources

www.goauthentic.org

Published by Earthwhile Publishing
PO Box 77
Westifled, IN 46074-0077

Library of Congress Cataloging-In-Publication Data

Haddix, John

The Authentic Musician: Discovering Your Purpose As An Artist

ISBN- 978-0-578-05442-1

Editor: Janet Schwind
Photography: Cathy Howie
Cover Design: Tomas Howie

Printed in the United States of America

Acknowledgements

This book is written with unending appreciation to all those who've poured into my life the love, truth and grace of God either by their words, gifts or example. Special thanks go to my parents, my music teachers and spiritual mentors. Countless people have impacted my life over the thirty plus years of music ministry and I'm thankful for each musician, artist and tech person I've been able work with. Writing this book has been an adventure. I'm especially thankful for our supporters who've stood by us in our work, enabling me to write and serve God's Kingdom. Thanks also goes to Janet Schwind who diligently edited my manuscript and Tom and Cathy Howie (www.halcyonarts.org) for their wonderful photography and cover design.

My most indebted love and appreciation go to my amazing wife, Pam, and our two wonderful daughters, Lindsy and Krista. I am humbled to live each day with such a wonderful woman, authentic artist and worshipper as my wife! Her insight, patience and love are all over this project!

This book is dedicated in loving memory of my parents, Lewis and Roberta. Their love for God, their family and music continues to echo through our lives.

The Authentic Musician

Contents

Introduction..9

1. What is an "Authentic Musician"?...............................13

2. Raising the Bar – Skill development.............................25

3. Discovering and Guarding your Heart..........................41

4. What's the Point of Music Anyway?.............................61

5. Relating to Other Artists: Comparing, Competing and
Contributing..83

6. Me? Impact People Through Music?............................91

7. Off-stage Authenticity..115

9. Sanity...137

10. Leaving an Authentic Trail.......................................153

11. Postlude..169

Appendix..173

Believing in God and Beginning a Relationship............175

Leading Artists..193

Resources to Grow By...211

Quotes to Ponder:...213

Notes:..215

Introduction

Music. Chances are, you started enjoying music while you were in your mother's womb or shortly after you entered this world. Especially in our modern culture, music can infiltrate just about every space of life—even the delivery room! And you find it enjoyable—at least, your type of music. And I assume that since you are reading this, you want to be a better musician/artist or help someone who does, or you just want to understand artists better. (That's a challenge!)

Regardless, being an artist not only involves your gift or ability but also a determination to develop that gift. And the moment you decided to take your development seriously, you began a *journey*! If your journey has been anything like mine, you know it has been at times fun, exciting and fulfilling; and other times drudgery to very discouraging. You may have even given up. You also know that whether you have a lot of natural abilities or a small amount, you can always develop your abilities further both for your own enjoyment and the enjoyment of others. There's always room for grow for even the most accomplished artists!

My desire in this book is to try to help you move *forward* as a artist—to not only understand the *how* but also the *why* of that challenge. As you read, you may be surprised to discover what is holding you back, or you may discover some new ideas that will help you improve your abilities and help those you play with. Hopefully, you will find both!

My Journey

Music was a very natural part of my life growing up. We had a piano in our house, and it was always there inviting me to sit down and play it. So, I started playing it probably before I could swing a bat, cast a fishing line or say a complete sentence. But I found that when I played, my ears were pleased! (I was probably the only one in our house who thought this.) I discovered there was something about being able to express myself musically that was very gratifying. I also found that music can be a means to gain acceptance by others. I had an older brother who was an excellent pianist, and I saw the affirmation he got as a result. So, true to my human nature, I also started to play not only for my pleasure but to seek the affirmation of others. It was also a means for me to serve other people, whether it was providing entertainment at a club or a processional at a wedding. And because that worked pretty well for me most of my growing up years, I pursued developing my gifts.

I suspect you have a similar story. I believe that acceptance, affirmation, service and self-expression are at the heart of most artistic motivation. But, in my late teens, I began to grow dissatisfied with my motivations. I found that those things, of themselves, still left an emptiness and provided inadequate motivation to keep growing and pushing myself. I also found that when I failed to impress people musically or when I was "dry" in my musical creativity, I became discouraged. At that point I faced a decision to either give up or pick up and keep trying to learn and grow. To do nothing meant to retreat. Sometimes it meant taking extra lessons, or researching more, or practicing more. Sometimes I needed to "chill out" and get refreshed for a

Introduction

while too. But it always meant trying to learn from my past and apply new lessons.

It was at that time—basically during my early 20s—when I also began to discover the elements of what I call an "authentic" or "total musician." And I've found since then that as I keep building on those elements, my playing and writing are driven by more than self expression and a fear of rejection. The results can be true fulfillment as a musician and hopefully a life of positive impact on the world and fellow musicians. It is my aim to share with you in a clear way the elements that serve as foundational building blocks for a fulfilling life as a musician.

It is not always easy to confront or accept some of these elements personally. They may call for a change in your thinking or approach to your playing, or even your life! Is that any surprise though? Just a quick look at the sports world reveals that athletes deal with much more than just the athletic skills needed for their performance. They often must look at their whole approach to life mentally, physically and even spiritually, to get the added 10% they're looking for. The same is true for musicians. Perhaps you're at a hurdle in your life that you just can't seem to get past. Perhaps you're stuck. Or maybe you're having a blast and just want to keep growing. Wherever you are, you can always move forward.

And the journey continues... overcoming roadblocks, conquering challenges, impacting others and expressing your heart! Being an artist is a unique calling. Developing yourself to your potential is a great challenge. May you take it on today!

Note: Musicians, artists, and players—those are words I use interchangeably. If you're a vocalist, instrumentalist, director, composer, artist, or something else artistic, please know that I'm including you in those thoughts. In the spirit of efficiency, please forgive my not making those distinctions every time I refer to an artist.

1. What is an "Authentic Musician"?

"Becoming an authentic person will give you the resources to create authentic art—art that fulfills you and impacts others."

Musicians come in all shapes and sizes, styles and capacities, colors and nationalities. Music is found in every culture and time in history, and so are musicians. So what is an authentic musician? We could define it as a musician who authentically plays the style of music they're attempting to play. In other words, they don't fake it! (i.e., an authentic jazz musician actually improvises on his instrument; he doesn't just copy someone else.) But besides being authentic stylistically, an *authentic* musician is an authentic or *real person* who doesn't hide behind a mask, someone who understands there's a purpose for his art and his life. They live out of that purpose and find fulfillment in doing so. You may or may not believe that people were created for a purpose. But if indeed a loving God has created us for a purpose, then it follows that we will find our greatest fulfillment and be most authentic in the *accomplishment* of our purpose. An authentic musician is first of all an authentic person.

This idea of purpose and design is not new. We see it everywhere. For instance consider a boat on a trailer. It isn't until the boat is launched off the trailer into the water with fuel and a driver that it actually fulfills its purpose. It was designed for the water and, in a sense, we would say that it really isn't fulfilled or "being an authentic boat" until it is zooming around the lake. To just keep the boat in the garage for storing stuff wouldn't make for an exciting or authentic "boat life!" Taking this a step further we could compare the type of boat it is to our individual artistic gifts. If it's a rowboat, it must not be used to pull skiers or head across the ocean. On the other hand, I grew up fishing and trust me, speedboats or ocean vessels don't make great fishing boats. Each boat is "gifted" with certain attributes that make it perfect for a particular purpose. As human beings with a creator/designer God, it's similar though of course much more complex. Our lives can be an ongoing, exciting discovery of both our loving God and unique purpose.

The dictionary defines *authentic* as: *Conforming to fact and therefore worthy of trust, reliance, or belief.* So what's an authentic person? *An authentic person is someone who has discovered the truths (facts) of who they were created to be and lives them out.* It means being the "real thing," the real person you were created to be. And being real is something we all long for in others and ourselves. Anyone who has studied the arts at all realizes it's not just the artist's art or outward expression of his gifts that matters or moves him to keep creating or growing. It's the *person* behind the art that determines whether there will be any further development or expression. It's the person behind the art that is often reflected (not always) in their art, and their "realness" gives their art credibility. I think we all know there are times when we sense there is something more. *Becoming an authentic person will give you the resources to create authentic art—art that fulfills you and impacts others.*

What is an "Authentic Musician"?

It's probably clear to you now that I am writing from some presuppositions based on what I believe are intellectually honest and reliable facts or truths of life. Two of my presuppositions are that: 1) we all were created by a loving and personally involved Creator, and 2) everyone and everything has been given a purpose. *If this is true, as I said earlier, then people will only find their greatest potential and fulfillment by discovering this Creator and His purpose for their lives.* Accordingly, when we stray from our purpose, what often appears to bring life actually brings death, because it's like putting a square peg in a round hole. It's like using a car as a tractor or as your bedroom, rather than for its intended use, taking people from place to place. It's an inauthentic use of the car. Not living out what you were made for results in disconnected living, frustration and despondency.

Despondent Artists

There are many examples of musicians and artists who, due to their *inauthenticity* as people, gave up or cut short their artistic lives and in many cases their very lives. Failing to know their life's purpose and often searching in the wrong places, they were left with little or nothing to live for. Here are a few examples.

Kurt Cobain, musician: As the successful lead singer and guitarist for the rock group Nirvana, his descent into self-destruction accelerated in 1994 as he went into a coma during tour dates in Italy (widely believed to be a failed suicide attempt) before returning to Seattle where he shot himself on April 5, 1994. He was 27.[1]

Tom Evans, musician: Commercial success proved elusive in the '80s and in November 1983, history repeated itself in the most bizarre scenario possible when singer/songwriter Tom Evans of Badfinger committed suicide [by hanging] at his Surrey(London) home at the age of 36. Like former band member, Pete Ham he had been suffering from depression and financial worries. The Badfinger story is uniquely tragic and among its greater ironies is the now morbid chorus of the song with which Pete Ham, who also committed suicide, and Tom Evans are best associated: "I can't live, I can't live anymore" (Without You)[2]

Vincent van Gogh, artist: In the last two years of his life, van Gogh also executed a number of self-portraits; had a brief, turbulent friendship with artist Paul Gauguin (they were roommates until one final argument took place) veered in and out of madness (institutionalizing himself from time to time); and continued to have a disastrous love life. In a bungled suicide attempt, he shot himself on July 27th, 1890, but didn't die until two days later. Vincent van Gogh died having sold one painting in his lifetime.[3]

We could go on and on with examples of depressed, despondent and suicidal artists. I recognize that sometimes there are physiological causes for these behaviors; on the other hand, it is not surprising that artists can become depressed because they seek to understand and reflect life in this world... and this world has problems. Without knowing hope beyond this world, depression and discouragement can often result. Much has been written on this, and if this is a curious point for you I would point you to authors like Francis Schaeffer, C.S. Lewis, Os Guiness, Philip Yancy and Lee Strobel. (See appendix)

For many of these despondent artists, their art may have reflected their heart at one point—that they were on a journey, seeking, growing etc.—but the absence of *discovering* true meaning and purpose as a person eventually left them empty or despondent. It is heart breaking to see. *And for each of the extreme examples like those above, there are countless numbers of other artists who simply died on the inside and gave*

What is an "Authentic Musician"?

up using their gifts, and perhaps gave up on what they hoped life would bring. If you've been around for any time at all, you've seen this type of painful and purposeless living among artists.

There are also those artists who have remained true to their artistic expression throughout their lives, but as they've continued to express their heart through their gifts it has revealed a great amount of hopelessness and defeat. Again, these are road signs of the lifelessness they are experiencing on the inside (if they are being honest in their art). While we commend them for their honesty, it is clear they haven't discovered the answers to their deepest needs, for which I believe there are answers.

Driven Artists

Is an authentic artist a driven artist? Maybe yes, maybe no. It depends on what is really driving them, and that is a heart issue. Sometimes drivenness is simply a passionate pursuit of a calling, or a creative outburst. The fruit of these outbursts is often amazing. Handel's writing of *Messiah* might qualify for this and many other creations. But when the drivenness has "bad fruit"—e.g., damaged relationships, selfishness, and egomania—we have to conclude that at least part of that drivenness is wrong. We'll look into this more in Chapter 3.

My Story

I found myself in my teenage years as a driven artist, but for some unhealthy reasons. I based my self-worth on my performance and I was driven by a fear of rejection. I also didn't know what I really believed. I knew it wasn't enough for me simply to follow what I had been raised to believe. While that may have been easier and worked for a previous generation (though not really), the world was changing and challenging my beliefs. I was struggling to see how it all fit together—if it did at all.

The Authentic Musician

Music was one means I had to express that longing. It also became a means for me to gain the acceptance and friendships I longed for. I thought that if I could just be good enough musically, I would feel loved and accepted. *Was the answer to my needs just in being a successful musician? Was that where true meaning and significance could be found? If I hit the "big time" would that fulfill my longings--my heart needs?*

I began to see that no, it would not. From observing other musicians and non-musicians, I began to believe that most people don't live with an adequate answer to life's greatest questions—questions every human being asks at some point in their lives. The downside was that I began to see that no matter how successful I would become as an artist, my heart would still have needs—needs I couldn't expect "success" as an artist to meet. The good thing, however, was that *I was beginning to realize the need to ask questions.* I realized that just to follow the status quo or the typical road map to success was not going to answer the needs of my heart. No matter how good I was as a musician, I knew something was missing and I began a search.... and I'm still searching on some levels. I find the pull and promise of our culture is always there that says real fulfillment is found in being rich, famous or powerful. On the basic level of my life, however, I've begun to discover the answers to my deepest needs for meaning and significance—the keys to authentic living. And it burdens me when I see others who are living totally disconnected from experiencing an authentic life.

This is part of the reason I feel compelled to write this book. The typical road map of a serious musician is to pursue success either in the music industry or in education, and to leave their questions behind. A friend of mine commented once on our "system" of handling musicians: "We all love music and pursue being musicians, and then all we do is become teachers so we can turn all of the younger musicians into teachers; it's a vicious circle!" A bit overstated, but if we become teachers simply because we think it's the only way to "do music" we've missed something. When we believe that, as I said earlier, often we just give up and settle for "less than" type of living. We assume there is no real significance or purpose to our music and even to our life. There *is* a great need for teachers but there is a greater purpose to our music than just teaching. Performing and teaching are good for what they are, but they alone won't provide true fulfillment. There is a higher purpose for our lives and our art. I hope in the next few chapters to help you ask questions not only about your musicianship but also about your heart. *I believe that if your heart is on the right journey, your art will begin to take on a new type of significance as well. It will help you move from surface expression to authentic expression.*

Once a fellow player at a gig challenged me to think about all the people we were playing for. He asked questions like, "What are these people really here for? Is there any purpose for their lives? Is there more than just living for the next party?" His questions got me thinking and asking more questions. And I've never stopped.

What about you? Have you begun to ask the deeper questions of the heart? Have you begun to discover what it means to truly be an authentic artist? Are you beginning to live out of the original purpose for which you were created? Are you pursuing being an authentic musician? If the examples of other artists are any clue, it is a critical journey worth taking, whether you are 15 or 55. To get us started, here are three critical components of being an authentic artist.

Marks of an Authentic Musician: Gifting, Skill and Heart

Gifting

Authentic musicians or artists have a *natural* talent for music or their art. Now it's very clear that everyone has certain gifts and talents—

and varying degrees of them. Your gifting is unique to you and you have a unique contribution to make. But first you must discover and discern your gifts. You may even learn new things about yourself even as you get older.

It's always healthy from time to time to sit back and assess what you've learned about your strengths and weaknesses, gifts and uniqueness, so that you can be wise about where you put your energy.

In my case, I grew up with a somewhat musical family where singing was common and a piano was always available. I also had a brother who was a rather accomplished pianist, and parents and grandparents who had some musical gifts, though not professional. As I watched others play and I listened, it was natural for me to want to play, and it was somewhat enjoyable. Of course, it was also frustrating to play because of my lack of skill and training early on. I also discovered as time went on that while I had a good ear, I was naturally stronger as an instrumentalist than vocalist. In high school I was intrigued by writing music and began to write big band and pop arrangements. I think the direction I went with my gifts could have been different had I been in a different musical environment (e.g.. strings, drums), but the basic ear and passion was there from the beginning.

Discerning Your Giftedness

So what about you? Do you have a clear assessment of your musical or artistic gifts? Perhaps you would do well to consider this. Be careful not to think of your skill development here. The question is, do you have artistic gifts? If so, what are they? It can be a painful realization for someone to find out they really aren't as gifted to play, sing, write or draw as well as they thought—even though they may be putting more sweat, blood and tears into their development than anyone else. The problem may not be their motivation or discipline at all, but simply their giftedness. Then there are also those who have multiple gifts of playing, singing and writing. Their challenge is deciding what gifts to develop. The sooner you realize where you are and are not gifted, the sooner you can be on the path to focusing your efforts as an artist. Is there a timeline to all of this? Not really; it depends on the opportunities you've had to discover your gifts. People like Mozart discovered their gifts at a very young age (with help from his father and others). As well, there are people who've picked up an instrument late in life and made amazing progress. The aptitude was there all along, but the opportunity or motivation was not realized until later.

Shows like *American Idol* and *America's Got Talent* demonstrate to us both of these issues. Some people are harshly rejected and surprised to find out that they are not as gifted as they thought. For others, it is amazing to see how far they can grow and develop over the course of the competition. (I advise getting some honest and professional feedback before trying out for these shows unless you want to end up on the outtakes.)

Every artistic discipline requires basic innate gifts unique to each craft, whether drama, dance, vocal, instrumental, art or video, etc. I encourage you to ask some honest friends, a mentor or a teacher about this. Be willing to hear affirming and non-affirming comments, knowing that once you have an accurate assessment, you can focus on your strongest gifts. I doubt that there has ever been an accomplished artist who has not had the affirmation, insight and encouragement of multiple mentors. If you don't have confidence in your gifting and potential, you will be very demotivated to grow. If on the other hand you have an accurate and positive assessment of your gifts by yourself and others, you will find the vision and motivation to grow and create something valuable!

Usually the wisdom you gain over time from your experience, others' feedback and your "joy factor" will affirm to you if you are gifted in an area.

We'll tackle the remaining marks of an Authentic Artist in the next two chapters.

So what's the answer to the question, "What's an authentic musician?"

*An authentic artist is someone who knows his **giftedness**, develops his **skill**, and creates his art with a growing," spiritually alive" **heart**.*

What is an "Authentic Musician"?

Follow-up Questions

Chapter One: What Is an Authentic Musician?

1. If an authentic musician is, first of all, an authentic person, how would you rate yourself when it comes to the discovery of your life's purpose and significance? (1 = not a clue, to 10 = well on the journey of understanding)

2. How well would you say you are living from your heart as an artist? In other words, are you living authentically? (never, sometimes, most of the time, always)

3. The three marks of an authentic artist are gifting, skill and heart. What would you say are your artistic gifts? (Be as specific as possible.)

4. What have others affirmed in you – besides those who just say it because they love you? ☺ (i.e., from people who know what they're talking about)

5. Your motivation to grow musically/artistically is: bottomed out, struggling, okay, growing, all-time high. Why?

The Authentic Musician

2. Raising the Bar – Skill development

"Do you see a man skillful in his work? He will stand before kings..."
Proverbs 22:29

How about your development? Are you growing as a guitar player, writer, pianist, singer, dancer, artist, actor, filmmaker, video artist, etc.? You believe you have some artistic gifts, now what's holding you back?

Good Mentors Are Essential

The one essential key that all of us need at some point is a coach or teacher—a person to help us actually do the work and hold us accountable as well as give us feedback and training. Talk to any accomplished artists and they will point to several people who've helped or influenced them to grow. And chances are, they're still learning and growing from others! There are also more resources than ever available to us, thanks to technology and the many artists who've gone before us and shared their wisdom. Understanding this, here are some other points for you to consider.

Barriers Are Inevitable

You've been playing for a while and the "honeymoon" phase of your playing is over. The honeymoon may have been just getting an instrument in the first place or maybe having a new improved instrument, or getting lessons from that sought-after teacher. But now reality hits and your expectations have deflated; you've hit a barrier. Barriers come when you find you still can't play those licks, or sing that style or get that sound you want. And then there are the times when you aren't the only one who notices you've hit the wall, or you hear someone else who is miles ahead of you and you think, What's the use?

Barriers can do that. They can hit us emotionally and be very discouraging. They can make us feel like we will never progress. On the other hand, the challenge of overcoming barriers can be invigorating. So, how do we handle them? Sometimes, it's good to address the emotional side. Reading or watching stories of other artists or athletes who have overcome barriers can be motivating. Better yet, hanging out with some "overcomers" may cause their attitude to rub off on you. The first decision any overcomer makes is to tackle the barrier believing that the "pain is worth the gain."

Rudy, We Are Marshall, My Left Foot, Rocky, The Pursuit of Happyness and many other movies and books carry this same theme of overcoming obstacles and people becoming stronger in the process. Let yourself be inspired by these stories, especially the ones based on real people.

Why Raise the Bar?

"Without an adequate answer to the question 'why should I do it?' we won't run the extra lap, we won't say no to the extra piece of cake..."[4] *(Bob Biehl consultant)*

The first question you have to address in overcoming barriers is why. Why do you want to improve or even stay in the scene? If you don't have a goal or a vision (picture of your future) that you believe in, you won't give it your best and you won't be willing to sacrifice for it. It's as simple as that. All of us are motivated to do things that are easy and hold treasure at the end. It's when it gets tough, however, that our motivation and commitment are tested, and we either re-ante up or bow out. The question is, Do you have an adequate reason in front of you to press through the difficult times? Note, too, that in the long run of *lifetime* development, it will take a *strong* motivation to sustain you.

This is what separates the average, mediocre player from the achiever. And whether you start out highly motivated or not, eventually your motivation and commitment (combined with your gifting and training) will determine your success. *What is it these days that motivates you to improve?* Why do you want to raise the bar? Is it enough to keep you going when it gets rough? If not, how can you "stoke" the flame of your motivation or redefine your vision? As I mentioned earlier, for me the answer to that changed in my 20s. I found myself redefining my major motivation and vision. My old reasons for pursuing growth became inadequate.

It's important to realize there is an intellectual and an emotional side to any change—and overcoming barriers represents change! In fact, as Chip and Dan Heath comment in their book *Switch*, it is actually better to think not of raising the bar but lowering it by breaking your challenge into small steps you can practically tackle, thus giving your emotional side the motivation it needs to go for it.

In their book, the Heaths in their book point out a proven method for making difficult changes in our lives, which also applies to overcoming an artistic barrier. They use a three-point strategy likened to a man riding on an elephant. How do we move forward? By addressing these elements of our lives:

1. Direct the Rider – Our *minds* must be convinced this is a change we need to make and it should make sense, be reasonable.

2. Motivate the Elephant – Our *emotions* must be encouraged to feel the benefit of the change. This is one reason small steps and rewards are important.

3. Clear the Path – Identify things that make your process more difficult than it needs to be; for instance, perhaps practicing your instrument while also answering emails will distract you from concentrating on your playing.

Here are more thoughts from some proven "motivation gurus."

"Hold a picture of yourself long and steadily enough in your mind's eye, and you will be drawn toward it." – Napoleon Hill [5] *, author, lecturer.*

"The whole idea of motivation is a trap. Forget motivation. Just do it. Exercise, lose weight, test your blood sugar, or whatever. Do it without motivation. And then, guess what? After you start doing the thing, that's

when the motivation comes and makes it easy for you to keep on doing it."– John C. Maxwell [6], author, pastor, motivational speaker.

"There's always the motivation of wanting to win. Everybody has that. But a champion needs, in his attitude, a motivation above and beyond winning. "– Pat Riley [7] NBA coach.

The Process of Overcoming Barriers

Okay, assuming your why question is *adequately* answered, how do you beat your barriers? You must identify your barriers, focus your attack, evaluate your progress, and be persistent and disciplined while also maintaining other areas of your craft.

Identify your barriers

The first step is to clearly identify your barrier or barriers. Just like most any problem, there are symptoms and then there are root causes. The point here is to attack the root cause. For instance, when I was learning trumpet, like most trumpeters, I wanted to play high and I thought that meant straining my throat and pressing the horn into my face to squeak out those notes. But, it wasn't until I really worked on my breath support that I started to see lasting success. My root problem was having adequate support.

Often it takes a teacher or mentor to help you with this. We often have bad habits we are not even aware of that an outside observer can easily identify. The investment of a good teacher can save you hours of frustration and quickly help you identify your real barriers.

Here are a few of the basic issues/barriers you may need to consider:

Posture

Breath support (vocalists, wind players)

Tension in your throat or shoulders, etc.

Hand/Arm position (instrumentalists)

Practice technique

Learning more about your craft

Planning your development

Here are some you may not have considered:

Muscle strength

Just like an athlete you have to develop your muscles and this usually means repetition or practice—and not just showing up to do it, but showing up to accurately do it! The phrase "practice makes perfect" is only partially true. On the other hand "perfect practice makes perfect—or at least it makes for the greatest improvement" Sometimes your progress may seem to be slow. Anyone who has lifted weights knows that the jump from pressing 100 to 200 lbs takes a lot of time and repetition. On the other hand if you are seeing some progress, even a little, let that encourage you to press on. This may require that you focus on certain muscle groups depending on your instrument. If you think about what specific muscles you use to play or sing, exercising or resting them specifically will make them grow. Exercise specifically for specific results. On the other hand cross-training can have some benefits too, just like sports. Depending on your instrument, strengthening arms and shoulders may help you gain greater endurance and posture. Sometimes just the discipline of physical exercise can help you take the "discipline mindset" over to your practicing.

Raising the Bar – Skill development

Fitness

Your whole body is involved in whatever you do. (I'm great at stating the obvious! "Wherever you are, there you are.") Therefore, how you take care of your body has a direct impact on your playing. Cardio exercise can have a big impact on your lung capacity and alertness. Plus, getting enough sleep and a good diet are huge too. If you're a vocalist, be aware also that certain foods may contribute to your vocal or sinus problems. For instance caffeine drinks can cause sinus drainage, which can interfere with your voice as well as dehydrate your throat. Juices and dairy products can also cause mucus problems, which affect your vocal chords.

Regular practice

There is no substitute for disciplined practice. If you are easily distracted, make sure:

- You have specific goals written down for each week.
- Create as best you can an undistracted environment; remove the TV, computer, phone, and whatever else will keep you from staying focused on your task.
- Pick the best time possible for your practice, a time when you are alert and able to really focus.
- Invite someone to hold you accountable, to check in with weekly or daily on your practice schedule or goals. For many of us, it was our mom or a friend who held us to our commitment. This can also mean joining a band or other group that will keep pushing you and challenging your level of playing.
- Expose yourself to other players and learn from their playing and practice habits.
- Listen, listen, listen to other artists, live and recorded
- Record yourself and evaluate your playing or singing.

The Authentic Musician

Attitude

Could your greatest barrier be your attitude? Charles Swindoll, a favorite author of mine says, "Attitude is everything." Your attitudes are made up of your thoughts and emotions and are outwardly expressed in your words, expressions and posture. Now when it comes to your musical barriers, what are your attitudes? When it comes to practice, what's your attitude? Here are just a few I've noticed over the years. I think the differences are obvious:

Defeatist - I can't do this, why even try? I'll never improve.

Unbeliever - I'll do it, but it won't help. When will this lesson/practice time be over?

"Complier" (compliant type) – Okay, I'll work on this for you (parent, teacher, whomever). When will you leave me alone?

Competitor - I'm going to beat him/her next time, and then I'll be respected, and accepted, worth something.

Pursuer - I'm thankful for my unique gifts, and I'm going to keep developing them to their greatest potential so I can make my greatest contribution to my team, my listener's enjoyment and myself.

I'm sure there are many other possible attitudes. But the point here is to monitor your attitudes. They have a huge impact on your progress. What are your thoughts as you face your barriers? What is your self-talk? Why do you feel that way? Who or what are you believing about yourself and your abilities/potential? If you have a bad attitude when you're practicing or facing a barrier, it's time to stop and correct your thoughts and perspective. How we do that could take another book to explain, but the quick answer is that you need to tackle the *thoughts* you're allowing into your mind and to exchange them with "mind renewing" thoughts. Be careful of what (or whose) words you allow to

32

influence you, and let your mind dwell on positive, hopeful, truthful thoughts.

It is also important to remember the reward you feel when you overcome a barrier. Many times remembering your reward will keep you going through the rough times. Again: "Without an adequate answer to the question of why, the cost is always too high." In other words, you must believe that the price you are paying to improve will be worth it! If you don't believe, you won't achieve. Your attitudes are a reflection of your thoughts and values, which come from your heart. We must always guard our attitude when we face barriers. As Charles Swindoll said, "The remarkable thing is, we have a choice every day regarding the attitude we will embrace for that day."[8]

Focus your attack

Once you have identified your root barrier(s), the next step is to seek the best exercises that will start to break the old habit and develop the new. Again, this is often greatly aided with a teacher or mentor who may know exactly what you should do. You can also research for yourself on the Internet (e.g., YouTube) and possibly find the right formula to help you break through your musical barriers. After that, it will take FOCUSED practice. Again, old habits are hard to break. If you practice correctly, eventually the new habits will become natural and you will find yourself rising to the next level of playing or singing—which is usually exhilarating!

Focused goal setting and disciplined practice may even take you beyond your finish line. Just like the athletes who make an extraordinary catch or hit a winning home run, when asked if they're surprised they often say "no" because they have practiced their exercises or routines to the point where certain skills and attitudes are almost second nature.

Baby steps

You will become overwhelmed if you try to tackle all of your barriers at once. Sometimes it will seem impossible for you to overcome them. That's when you have to remember that every big accomplishment is made up of little accomplishments along the way. If you keep practicing correctly, you will see progress. The key is to look back and see the progress you've made over time and to celebrate even the little victories. As the old saying goes, "How do you eat an elephant? One bite at a time!"

We tend to have our expectations set too high for the short-term and too low for the long-term. The distance between our expectations and future reality is usually our disappointments. If you keep your short-term expectations low enough, you will realistically see progress and may even surprise yourself. At the same time, keeping your long-term goals high and pushing yourself to pursue them by stretching yourself to the next short-term goal may result in reaching your goals even earlier than you planned! In other words, make your short-term goals realistic, reachable and rewarding while keeping a long-term vision in front of you.

And what if, once you've completed your normal practice, you took another 10 minutes to practice scales or theory, or read? Doing just that little bit more will probably accelerate your pace. The sports world again gives us lots of examples of athletes who did that little bit above and beyond the normal workout, and that little bit eventually put them ahead of their peers.

Evaluate

You must take time to evaluate your progress and the effectiveness of what you're doing. To not do so is to risk heading in the wrong direction. You may be familiar with the saying attributed to Albert Einstein, that "Insanity is doing the same thing over and over, expecting different results." This applies to practice in the sense that if you don't evaluate your strategy to see if it's producing the progress you want, you might be just spinning your wheels. Of course you must give adequate time for any exercise to have an effect, but if you are seeing no progress over time, it may be time for a change. Again, this is where private lessons with a good mentor or teacher are indispensible. Having an objective source to evaluate your progress greatly helps. It is also very important to update your short-term goals and keep moving toward a higher objective.

Persistence/Discipline

Persistence is crucial to seeing long-term progress. If you do the correct exercises the correct way long enough, there is a 99% chance you will see progress. If you don't see progress, either you have a physical barrier that can't be overcome, or you are working on the wrong problem!

There is no substitute for discipline. Even the very best artists still discipline themselves to certain regular routines to help them stay on top of their game. The instrumentalists still run their scales, vocalists still vocalize, writers still write. The story goes that a famous piano virtuoso was once asked why he practiced so much. Every day he could be heard practicing scales and compositions. He answered, "If I miss one day of practice, only I notice it. If I miss two days of practice, my colleagues notice. And if I miss three days, my audience notices!"

Disciplined practice is probably the biggest factor between a good player and an expert. Author Daniel J. Levitin comments concerning recent studies about "expert" performers:

Anders Ericsson, at Florida State University, and his colleagues approach the topic of musical expertise as a general problem in cognitive psychology involving how humans become experts in general. In other words, he takes a starting assumption that there are certain issues involved in becoming an expert at anything.... The emerging picture from such studies is that ten thousand hours of practice is required to achieve the level of mastery associated with being a world-class expert—in anything. In study after study of composers, basketball players, fiction writers, ice skaters, concert pianists, chess players, master criminals, and what have you, this number comes up again and again. Ten thousand hours is equivalent to roughly four hours a day for 5 days a week for ten years! It seems that it takes the brain this long to assimilate all that it needs to know to achieve true mastery.[9]

Please don't miss the point here. You may not desire to be an "expert" or to be "world class"; the cost on the surface may be inconceivable to you. But if you want to have any level of proficiency, it will require practice. Anyone would agree that looking at 10,000 hours of practice is overwhelming if they don't see the progress and joy in the process. And often this is not a conscious decision many artists made at the beginning of their serious playing. Rather, they grew into it as they saw success and opportunity. If you're after becoming an "expert" as they define it, you must be convinced that this is a path you should take. The cost is high and, of course, the more effectively you practice, the faster you will grow!

"My attitude is never to be satisfied, never enough, never."
-Duke Ellington[10]

Maintain other areas

One point to remember is that while you want to focus on your growth area, you should also maintain other aspects of your playing too. If you don't keep a balance, you will find yourself slipping in other areas. For example, you should always warm up, practice scales, or whatever.

Raising the Bar – Skill development

Then as you see your barrier being overcome, maintain your overall progress by paying increased attention to other areas of your playing so you don't slip into some bad habits. For instance, if you're a horn player working on tonguing technique but neglecting your breath support or posture, you will handicap yourself from achieving your ultimate goal of good range and good tonguing technique.

What about you—specifically?

You may have noticed that I purposefully kept many of these points rather general and haven't talked about your specific instrument or ability. That is because you will have barriers or issues unique to your craft, or even your physiology, that would fill volumes to address. And as I said, there are lots of resources out there to help you *specifically*—books, Internet, teachers, classes, etc. The point, however, is that everyone faces barriers. If you are a serious musician, you will want to identify and overcome them. So go for it.... an authentic musician always strives to do his best and that is what excellence is all about. As you improve, you will raise the bar for yourself and inspire others around you to do the same. Skill development and maintenance is always on the list of goals for even the most accomplished artists. When your skills match your performance requirements, then the joy of playing and your impact will be multiplied.

In John Maxwell's book *Talent is Never Enough*, he highlights the following 13 points related to developing our skills.

1. Belief lifts your talent
2. Passion energizes your talent
3. Initiative activates your talent
4. Focus directs your talent
5. Preparation positions your talent
6. Practice sharpens your talent
7. Perseverance sustains your talent

8. Courage tests your talent
9. Teachability expands your talent
10. Character protects your talent
11. Relationships influence your talent
12. Responsibility strengthens your talent
13. Teamwork multiplies your talent[11]

These are great insights and the book is a good resource. It also points to the fact that developing your skill is much more than just executing some techniques. It requires a lot of internal strength and motivation. The next chapter tackles the internal world of an artist and the beginning point of authenticity.

"You've got to learn your instrument. Then, you practice, practice, practice. And then, when you finally get up there on the bandstand, forget all that and just wail." *–Charlie Parker[12], jazz saxophonist*

Raising the Bar – Skill development

Follow-up Questions

Chapter Two: Raising the Bar: Skill Development

1. What teachers or coaches have been most influential in your development? Do you have or need a teacher/coach now? How should you pursue this?

2. When it comes to developing your gifts to the next level, do you feel motivated? Are your reasons strong enough to move you to at least take the first steps (finding a new teacher, practice time, etc.)? Why or why not?

3. Of the various barriers listed, which do you relate to? What are some other growth areas you need to tackle?

4. Which of the attitudes do you relate to the most? (Defeatist/ Unbeliever/Complier/Competitor/Pursuer)

5. What do you need to focus on most to make initial progress? When will you practice? Who will help hold you accountable?

6. What would you consider "baby steps" of progress? After accomplishing one step what would the next step be? (You may need help here.)

7. How will you practice so that you maintain other areas of your skill?

8. How will you reward yourself for your progress (short-term and long-term)?

The Authentic Musician

3. Discovering and Guarding your Heart

There's an old proverb that says, "Guard your heart with all diligence, for from it flow the springs of life"[13]

You need to give your heart some attention. If you want a continual flow of life and growth in your music or art, you need to give your heart some attention. If you want to push through the next barrier in your playing or writing, you need to give your heart some attention. If you want to have greater impact in others' lives through your art, you need to give your heart some attention.

In fact, your heart is *central* to your authenticity and it takes *continual* attention and nurturing. There are many reasons for this. Creating art, especially large works, can be very draining—emotionally, mentally, relationally, and even spiritually and physically.

Creating art always involves tension. Whether it's a story, a painting, a song or an album, there are a myriad of decisions to be made between beginning and ending, conflict and resolution, harmony and melody, evaluation, second-guessing, etc. For some artists it has driven them nearly crazy! The amount of energy it takes to create a large work is incredible and most non-artists have little understanding of all the time and energy that can go into creating even a small video piece, musical arrangement, painting or dance choreography. Sometimes it takes great vigilance to keep your work from becoming an unhealthy compulsion.

Displaying one's art requires vulnerability. It often takes great courage for an artist to share her work with even the most non-condemning audience, let alone other artists and critics! And if an artist is seeking to find her significance through others' affirmation or applause, she is set up for fear, disappointment, disillusionment and hurt. Plus, life is a battle. Often pressures from "life outside your art" can weigh on you, taking energy, motivation and time away from your creativity and growth. Of course, life also has seasons and there is an ebb and flow to creativity. But too often artists use this as an excuse to just give up altogether—a path they were never intended to take. Sometimes this battle is focused directly at your heart.

All of these pressures can leave your heart vulnerable to abuse and *unhealthy* shortcuts to rejuvenation. The point is that an authentic musician knows his heart is central to his success, and he knows he must regularly re-calibrate his heart to regain his motivation, contribution and perspective. The first step to rejuvenation is to initially discover (or rediscover) your true heart. *That is the challenge: to live from your heart! This is the only way to become the unique, authentic person you were created to be.*

Discovering your heart

What is your heart? It is the place of your will and deepest commitments, your emotions and thoughts. It is the seat of your conscience and the place where your true self resides. Many would also say it's the seat of artistic expression. The dictionary defines the heart as "the vital center and source of one's being, emotions, and sensibilities. The repository of one's deepest and sincerest feelings and beliefs. The seat of the intellect or imagination."[14]

42

Discovering and Guarding your Heart

Author John Eldredge puts it this way: "It [the heart] is the source of our faith, our hope, and of course, our love. It is the 'wellspring of life' within us, the very essence of our existence, the center of our being, the fount of our life. It is the connecting point, the meeting place between any two persons. The kind of deep soul intimacy we crave with God and with others can be experienced only from the heart."

He goes on to say that the heart is the source of our emotions, *but also much more than just emotions.* It is the location of our motives, our conscience, and our deepest thoughts. Courage and creativity come from our heart. It is who we are, the real self.

He concludes: "Of course your heart would be the object of a great and fierce battle. It is your most precious possession. Without your heart you cannot have God. Without your heart you cannot have love. Without your heart you cannot have faith. Without your heart you cannot find the work that you were meant to do. In other words, without your heart you cannot have life."[15]

This is why we must care for our heart!

Heart problems

I believe it is at the point of stress or emptiness where most people take a wrong turn. For most of us when we are close to empty or on empty—emotionally, creatively or spiritually—we turn to escapes or "quick fixes" that promise healing or rejuvenation but don't deliver. Our solutions may include vegging out on TV, or escaping to movies, shopping, sports, or drinking, and other more destructive escapes; I need not go on. Some of these things have their place and I'm not saying they're not helpful or all bad. The problem is that these are surface treatments. When we're drained we tend to look to surface things for refreshment, and none of them will deal with the deeper needs of our lives. In many cases, the surface things we seek not only *don't* fill us, but they deaden even further our motivations and attitudes. And often this "deadness" expresses itself in more self-destructive behavior or actions that hurt us and other relationships.

The source of life is in our heart. Unless we're willing to look "under the hood" the "blockage" or damage will continue, no matter how much surface living we do. We have to deal with our heart issues if we want to live authentically.

For me, realizing this has been a process. Early on, my answer to emptiness or exhaustion was to live off of others' approval or the next thing I could buy: "If I only had this or that, then I would be happy.." sort of thinking. In college I began to see that letting God speak to my heart was the only way I could experience forgiveness, freedom from the fear of rejection, and rejuvenation. I began taking time each day to be still and open my heart to God—to let Him speak to me from the Bible and others who I knew listened to Him. It was when I responded to what He spoke to my heart that I found life beginning to spring up. I know it sounds very mystical if you don't track with me on this, but for me this has been and continues to be very real. God revitalizes my heart! I'm not saying, however, that the answer is simply to listen to God. Knowing and listening to God from our heart is an unfolding journey of discovery that sometimes is easy and other times is very difficult, requiring a lot of humility, focus and attention. The fact is that our hearts have problems that can only be fixed by God.

God and Our Hearts

Why bring God into the picture? Only God, the creator of your heart, can show you and me the state of our hearts. One of the Bible's main artists, King David, said, "Search me, O God, and know my heart! Try me and know my thoughts! And see if there be any grievous way in me, and lead me in the way everlasting!" Ps 139:23, 24 The Bible explains that apart from God's grace, our hearts are lost and desperate for forgiveness and redemption (Romans 3:10-18, Jer 17:9).

How do we experience God's healing in our hearts? It begins with believing in Him personally. I'm not talking about religion. I'm not talking about cleaning up your act. I'm not talking about becoming a fanatic. I'm not even talking about going to church. I'm talking about a relationship with God that can change your heart—but only if you want. If you're struggling with the idea of a personal relationship with God, that's okay. I just ask that you keep seeking answers and not give up. It's a process, and God loves you more that you can imagine. We can't talk about having an authentic heart without listening to what our Creator says about it. Only the Creator knows the real purpose for His creation. Only God knows the real reason and unique purpose for which He created you. He is willing to speak to you, but first you need to make sure you have a relationship with Him. If you're not sure of what you believe or don't know if you have a relationship with Him, please look at Appendix 1: Believing God and Beginning a Relationship.

If you've begun a relationship with God through Christ, it's important to realize what God actually says about your heart. Christians often have never been told or have never discovered what God says about their heart. Many believe (or have been told) that their heart is "desperately wicked," citing passages in the book of Jeremiah. Or they believe their heart is constantly displeasing to God, referring to passages like Eph 5:5,6. The fact, however, is that those verses are talking about an unredeemed heart—a person who has not trusted in Christ and received the newness of life for which He died and rose again to give us. Note for example that the Ephesians passage 5:8 says, "For at one time you were darkness but *now* you are light in the Lord."

It is true that apart from the intervention of God's saving grace in our lives, our hearts are described as being "dead," "desperately wicked" and destined for eternal separation from God and others. That was our life before Christ. The non-Christian needs a new heart as spoken of in the book of Ezekiel. "And I will give you a new heart, and a new spirit I will put within you. And I will remove the heart of stone from your flesh and give you a heart of flesh" (Ez 36:26).

If you are a Christian, it is *not* your job to *overcome* your own heart of stone and put on a heart of flesh. Your job is to by faith receive the new heart God has given you and realize the heart of stone is nailed to the cross. We must rediscover this amazing truth again and again! The New Testament states that though we are born in death, we can be "reborn" to new life through Jesus Christ, now. "For the wages of sin is death, but the free gift of God is eternal life through Jesus Christ our Lord" (Rom 6:23)

The pathway to becoming an authentic (whole) person begins with accepting Christ as your personal Lord and Savior. This is just the beginning! When we accept Him, He begins the process of transforming us into the person we were originally created to be. As we cooperate with Him, we learn that we've moved from spiritual darkness to light—from a dead spirit and heart to a living spirit and a new heart. (Ez 36, 2; Cor 5:17) And as we learn to live from these amazing truths, we find our hearts being renewed as we experience the abundant, authentic life Christ promised (John 10:10). Let's look at this process a little more closely.

The Battle

Once you decide to live authentically, you will face a very real battle. Your adversary seeks to keep you and me in anything but the real life for which we were created. Again, John Eldridge says, "The Bible sees the heart as the source of all creativity, courage, and conviction." This creativity, courage and conviction is needed as Christians because we are in a battle.

The Bible is not shy about stating that we live in a world of spiritual warfare. Our enemies are the flesh, the world and Satan. The apostle Peter urges that "as sojourners and exiles to abstain from the passions of the flesh, which wage war again your soul" (1 Peter 2:11). The apostle John admonishes us not to love the "world"—the system of life under Satan's control that he uses to tempt us and turn us from God. (1 John 2:15,16, 2 Cor 2:11) . Peter warns us, "Your adversary the devil prowls around like a roaring lion, seeking someone to devour" (1 Peter 5:8). Jesus also affirms this when he says, "the thief (Satan) comes only to steal, kill and destroy. I came that they might have life and have it abundantly" (Jn 10:10).

Again, our battle is with desires or passions of our flesh, the world system and Satan and his demons. We're under attack whether we like it or not. As a believer, your heart will be under attack, but you also have the resources to overcome through Christ. Through the cross and resurrection, Jesus overcame these forces and He lives in you. Again, this doesn't mean that all will be rosy and conflict free. Don't let anyone tell you that. In fact, the battle often seems to increase as our eyes are opened to see what Christ has done. But we can take heart that "he who began a good work in you will bring it to completion at the day of Christ Jesus" (Phil 1:6). Indeed, most of the New Testament letters are written to instruct believers in how to overcome these forces and live victoriously in this world.

Non-believers are also in a battle, whether they know it or not. Apart from God's grace they don't have the spiritual resources like Christ-followers to be victorious. It is Satan's primary objective to keep non-Christians in the darkness, blinded in their minds from seeing the light of the "gospel of the glory of Christ" (2 Cor 4:4). For the believer Paul says,

"At one time you were darkness but now you are light in the Lord. Walk as children of light" (Eph 5:8, 9). To understand this more, do a study sometime on the New Testament verses having "now" in them. You will discover some amazing truths that are true "now"!

Darkness represents the lies we believe, resulting in actions that lead to spiritual death and separation from God's intimate presence in our lives. The Bible also says that those who are in the light are on a journey of ever-increasing "authenticity" or restoration to their created purpose (Rom 8:28). Here's how this plays out.

Three Experiences

The Bible identifies three types of people:
- those who live in darkness (spiritually dead)
- those who live in the light (authentic Christians, spiritually alive)
- those who, though alive in the light, choose to walk in the darkness (inauthentic Christians)

True Christ-likeness is not instantaneous in this life; it's an ongoing process that we can either cooperate with or resist. *Therefore, an authentic Christian isn't perfect but one who keeps getting up when he falls, keeps seeking to grow and to follow God. He responds to God's call for change with faith, obedience, love and hope. Authentic Christians are always "in process." This type of Christian is what "turned the world upside down" in the days of the early church. They were real.*

Inauthentic Christians

There are also believers who don't walk in the light—they're living inauthentic Christian lives. Either they really are not Christians at all (self-deceived), or they are resisting God's will for their life. People who are in this third category are under the greatest tension and conflict in their hearts. They're trying to live under the world's values and systems but know their identity and calling is in God's Kingdom, His values and purposes. They may be in total rebellion or just trying to live the Christian life in their own power, resisting the power and work of God's Spirit in their hearts. *These are the most miserable people!* They're using their gifts and bodies for death rather than life—for the world rather than the kingdom.

Inauthentic living always results in being a poor reflection of Christ to the world and is met with loving discipline on God's part. The saddest thing about inauthentic Christians is that they are missing the real life God offers and believe lies that block their movement toward Him. It's a miserable way to live. And unfortunately, this is how many Christians in the U.S. live! Too often we're content to live in this place for a season, rather than to do the *humbling* work of confession and repentance.

What about you?

Of the three types of people mentioned above, where do you find yourself? We are all on a spiritual journey—a journey that leads to finding our purpose and life in Him in deeper and deeper ways. Are you a Christian but walking in the darkness, or are you consistently walking in God's light? An authentic person is someone who lives for God's purposes and allows Him to change not just the spiritual area, but also every other area of their lives. God has a great adventure in store for us, but we will only experience it as we walk with Him.

If as a Christian, you find yourself living an inauthentic life, know that the Bible is very understanding but at the same time does not leave you to wallow in your inauthenticity. This is why the apostle John wrote: "If we claim that we experience a shared life with him and continue to stumble around in the dark, we're obviously lying through our teeth— we're not living what we claim. But if we walk in the light, God himself being the light, we also experience a shared life with one another, as the sacrificed blood of Jesus, God's Son, purges all our sin" (1 Jn 1:6).

What to Do

When we find ourselves living inauthentically, we must, 1) agree with (confess) what God says about us—our false beliefs, attitudes and actions, i.e. sins, 2) turn our hearts from our sins (repentance) to the forgiveness, life and peace God offers, and 3) surrender to His Spirit to live through and empower us (transformation). It's important to remember that for every sinful action, there is a positive or holy action that God calls us to live out in His Spirit's power. He calls us to move from lying to truth telling, from stealing to honest work, from sexual immorality to purity, from selfishness to love, etc.

Also behind our sins often are needs or wounds that drive us to sin. Sin is typically a shortcut offered by the world to meet a legitimate need. When you have trouble overcoming a particular temptation, think about what needs are driving you to sin. Ask yourself what lies you are believing that lead you away from God. I believe God wants each of us to walk in freedom from sin's power in our lives and to not give in to the temptations the world so deceptively places in our paths. But how? How do we turn from temptation? How do we walk more and more in the abundant life Jesus came to give us?

The Broken Artist

If you are serious about walking with God and enjoying the life He promises, you must face the reality of your brokenness. Let me explain. Jesus said, "If anyone wishes to come after Me, he must deny himself, take up his cross and follow me" (Mk 8:34). To follow Jesus you have to deny yourself—your ego, your flesh, your pride—all that opposes God's will in your life. Then take up your cross. The cross was an instrument of death in Jesus' day. In essence Jesus is saying we must die—die to our agenda, die to all that is of our flesh—and then follow Him. This act of denying death and ourselves is what we call brokenness. Brokenness is the state of admitting we cannot fix ourselves. It goes beyond just admitting to God that we've blown it or rebelled against Him (confession). It's surrendering ourselves, our pride, our ego or self-righteousness.

Brokenness means giving up on trying to fix our lives. It means letting go of the idea that we can apply a "formula" to overcome temptation even. Many times in Christian teachings, we offer some new approach or rules which when applied often lead us eventually back to the same sins! What's wrong? Do we just need another formula or Scripture to memorize, another software program to block porn or another accountability group to overcome alcohol or greed? These are all good things but they can miss the point of our deepest needs.

A Bible teacher once told me that if you want to find out what sin really is, to understand it better, don't go to someone who is a new Christian, who just came out of a sinful lifestyle. He said instead go to the "old saint" who has faced the deep realities of sin over a lifetime. He will see much more clearly what sin is and how it leads us away from God. What is it that a victorious Christian has learned? What is it that an overcoming addict has learned? (We're all addicts by the way—addicts to sin.) It is that we have to get to the point of humility and brokenness over our failures and realize our desperation for God. We have to get to the point of letting the Healer touch our hearts—our woundedness, our dark memories or experiences. We need to allow Him to deliver us and heal our hearts, canceling the footholds Satan may have gained in us.

The time will come when you will face your brokenness if you haven't already.

The Authentic Musician

Brokenness - My Story

In college I was a promising trumpet major. I receive a scholarship for being the top freshman trumpet player in the large program at Michigan State University. After my freshman year I went through an embouchure change (front teeth were capped for that purpose) that forever changed my enjoyment in playing and ranking as a player. It was very difficult as this "embouchure experiment" on my teacher's part and mine, turned into a three-year uphill battle with little improvement—at least from my perspective. I began to realize I was drawing my self-worth from what I was doing and the status I had among my peers. Through this I recognized my need to give up trying to control my life and to define it the way I wanted. I had to come to a place of brokenness if I was going to let God use me. This, I have found, is an ongoing process of letting go over and over again. It's so easy to draw my self-worth from what I do or what I produce. It's ingrained in my flesh to go there! But each time I turn from my pride and admit my brokenness and inability to "fix" myself, I find God's abundant grace waiting for me.

Another area of brokenness I experienced is one many men can relate to. As a teenager I was exposed to pornography through a man at work. Just 16 years old, I was very naïve and unprepared for the onslaught of this type of material not only from this man, but also from the youth culture of the '70s. I was also not a Christian and I unwittingly gave the enemy a foothold in my mind, which he would often use in the future to lead me away from Christ. The "fix it" mentality is very typical in this scenario. "Just stay away from the magazines" or " just put a block on your computer" were the usual tactics. But these self-help fixes alone only enticed my flesh to try to find a way around it. The flesh, by the way, loves rules like this because when we do "stay away" for instance, the flesh loves to pridefully boast in our righteousness. Or it seeks to find the loophole in the rule that will lead us back into the sin. The mindset of trying to fix it myself, of finding the right formula to live righteously, was futile.

The truth is that rules and boundaries do not "fix us." The only path to healing is to follow the Healer—to meet the Healer and in brokenness give up on ourselves, our methods, our plan and to by faith receive His healing. Isaiah 53 and 1 Peter 2 reminds us that it is "by His wounds that we are healed." Jesus offers this healing to us constantly, but we must constantly take our place of dependence and surrender to Him by faith to be healed. We must give up on ourselves and believe and receive the new heart and life He died to give us. Out with believing lies, in with believing the truth! Sometimes His path to healing us is also through others, but it's always with the heart of brokenness.

Have you come to this point of brokenness in your life? Does the battle feel real? How do you process Mark 8:34? (*"If anyone would come after me, let him deny himself, take up his cross and follow me."*) God will use our brokenness!

When I felt such a keen sense of loss over my trumpet playing in college, I was encouraged by reading about Moses and his staff—not his people but his shepherding staff. Before he met God, Moses' staff was merely a piece of wood to lean on and prod sheep with. After he met God, however, it became an instrument he used to demonstrate God's power and His purposes—even to bring healing. God took the staff far beyond what it was in just Moses' hands. Could it be that God does the same for us? He wants us to "let go" of our control (or worse, idolatry) of our art, and to surrender our gifts and our abilities to Him to use for His purposes. Back then, this picture excited me to think that God had even higher purposes for my life. Looking back now 30 years later, I have no regrets. Being used by God for His purposes is far better than what the world offers!

This story of brokenness is a journey and a battle having many twists and turns. The point I hope you get, however, is that an authentic Christian keeps growing and seeking to engage in the battle and the journey toward Christ-likeness. (I recommend the books *The Bondage Breaker* by Neil Anderson, *Waking the Dead* by John Eldredge, *The Pressure's Off* by Larry Crabb and *TrueFaced* by Thrall/McNicol/Lynch)

Authenticity

An authentic person is someone who is alive spiritually and is growing into the life for which she was created. An authentic person is someone who increasingly lives out who they really are in Christ. They haven't arrived yet (heaven), but they're growing toward it.

Here are some amazing truths from the Bible about your new heart from Christ:

- You have been made alive spiritually and totally forgiven of all sins (Col 2:13).
- You have been released from sin's power, which enslaved you, and you've been freed to obey God (Rom 6:11; 8:15)
- You have been given Christ's character to put on of compassion, kindness, humility, gentleness, patience, forgiveness, boldness, steadfastness, self-control, peace, goodness and love (Col 3:16, Gal 5:21,22).
- You have been given God's Spirit to empower you to live, to guide you, and help you grow (Jn 16:13, Acts 1:8, Titus 3:5,6).
- Your new heart has Christ's character, uniquely lived through your gifts, passions, abilities and personality (Heb 10:16, 1 Peter 2:9,10; 4:10).
- Your new heart desires God as your first love, loves others unconditionally and is victorious over Satan, the world and the flesh (Ez 36:26; Eph 1:3-12; 2:4-10).

Discovering and Guarding your Heart

As you absorb His Word you will discover more of the new identity and heart God has given you through Christ. You'll be able to live in more and more freedom from sin's power and become "fully alive" to reflect the life God created you for. As you continue to walk in the light, ask God to show you your unique gifts, talents and passions. He created you with a "glory" he wants you to reflect—a unique personality, gifting and talents through which God wants to be glorified. As you learn to fulfill your "glory" through Christ, you will be more and more authentic!

"The glory of God is man fully alive." --Saint Irenaeus

Nurturing and Guarding your Heart

As you continue discovering your heart and applying God's truth to your life, the battle to try to distance you and discourage you from His best will always be present. And the battle will always be aimed at your heart.

Some keys to fighting and winning the battle for God's best are:

- Fill your mind with truths from the Bible about God, your new identity and life in Christ and His ways. Replace wrong thoughts with Biblical truths and promises.
- Paul constantly talks about putting off the old self and putting on the new. This is a deliberate act of faith to receive what God says about you and to leave the old nature and lies behind.
- Take time for regular reflection (quiet times), community with other believers and prayer.
- Seek to be mentored by more mature believers.
- Monitor the effect different people and environments have on you. If you don't sense God's pleasure in your activities or relationships, it's time for a change.

Changed Hearts = Changed World

As a Christian you have a general calling to become like Christ in all you do. And you also have a specific, unique calling to be an influence in the world with your life, your gifts and your art. Ultimately the most authentic person ever was Jesus Christ, and He also had a specific job to do.

Lest you think all the talk about God means you should become "religious" and only do religious work and produce religious art, far from it! God really doesn't see the sacred and secular lines the church world has created. He sees it all and wants us to live all of our lives as an act of worship to Him, whether it's cleaning toilets, rehearsing in a small group or playing for a packed audience. As you continue to grow God will continue to work in your heart and reveal His call.

"Work out your salvation with fear (awe) and trembling, for it is God who is at work in you to will and to work for His good pleasure" (Phil2:13).

Becoming an authentic person not only changes your values and direction but it also changes your relationships. Sometimes your choice to be authentic will irritate and antagonize people toward you. But for those who choose authenticity, it will result in deeper and more fulfilling relationships than are otherwise possible. Authentic relationships take wisdom, work, time, insight, humility, prayer and oftentimes friction to grow deeply. Above all, we're called to pursue Christ-like love in our relationships. This is a big subject I will address later. It was the authentic *relationships* of the early church that turned the world around in that day. The same is possible today!

Discovering and Guarding your Heart

But What About the Arts?

An authentic musician is someone who knows his giftedness, develops his skill, and creates music with a growing, "spiritually alive" heart. But what about a musician's music? Where do music and the arts fit into an authentic person's life? We've already established that when we use music apart from its intended purpose (i.e., to gain fame, self worth, acceptance, etc.), we become inauthentic, which leads to emptiness. But, what is the proper place for music in a musician's life if it's not for all of these other things? How important should it be?

Again, we know for sure how important it should *not* be... It should not replace God in our lives. Sadly, for some artists, their art is clearly the most important thing in their lives—their god or idol. Or maybe it is an avenue to their "god" (money, sex, etc.) It comes down to understanding God's word: His purpose for the arts. We'll tackle that in the next chapter.

Endnote:

About Understanding the Bible: Convictions, Persuasions, and Opinions

It has been helpful for me to realize that the Bible is crystal clear on many issues and less clear on other less critical issues. It pleases God to show us the essential truths on many issues, but He has also given us the choice to decide what we believe on others. A friend has called these "issues of blood, pen or pencil"—convictions, persuasions and opinions. Issues the Bible is very clear on are matters of *conviction* (things you might be willing to sign in blood) such as the deity of Christ, the means of salvation, assurance of salvation, God's existence, the inspiration of Scripture, the Great Commission, etc.

On other issues the Bible leaves room for differing views, and you may have *persuasions* about these issues, such as the means of baptism, eternal security, or certain prophetic issues, etc. What's important is that

57

God doesn't want these issues to become divisive to your fellowship with other believers. They may determine the church you attend or your denomination, but you must still join hands with those who differ, that we might continue in God's main agenda for us of loving each other and reaching the world.

The third set of issues are *opinions*—issues on which the Bible has little to say and gives you freedom to choose. These include such things as style of music you listen to, movies you see, what you wear or places you go—things that are more cultural in nature. You must still steer away from immoral uses of these things, (like sexually explicit movies or clothing) and guidance comes more by principles from His word than outright statements of right or wrong. We are still accountable to God for our decisions in these areas and must let our conscience, God's Spirit and the Scriptures be our guide. The problem with many believers is that we tend to major on the minors and minor on the majors. We become judgmental of others on "pencil" issues and miss the bigger "blood" or "pen" issues where we should be focusing.

Another helpful study point has been that people's understanding of who God is in the Bible is progressive. Throughout biblical history, God increasingly revealed who He was over time. So people in the time of, say, Abraham did not have as much understanding of God as the early church. This is helpful in understanding the people's response to God and what God was teaching them. It also helps us realize the treasure and responsibility we have with the wealth of truth God has communicated to us through the Old and New Testament.

Discovering and Guarding your Heart

Follow-up Questions

Chapter Three: Discovering and Guarding Your Heart

1. Do you agree that your heart is central to your becoming an authentic person? Why or why not?

2. In what state would you put your heart these days? (Choose: Lost (post fall), Redeemed but faltering, or Redeemed and growing.

3. Do you agree with the first two beliefs (see appendix 1): "God is real" and "God has revealed truth to us"? Why or why not?

4. Believing God and His truth (the Gospel), accepting his offer for forgiveness and a personal relationship are the only way to know and experience the "new heart." Where in this journey are you? Where are you struggling? (It's not wrong to struggle; it's often a long process!)

5. Of the three types of people mentioned below, where would you put yourself?

    ➢ Living in darkness
    ➢ Living in the light
    ➢ Living in the light but walking in the dark

6. What one step can you take to help you go deeper and live more from your new heart? (Suggestions: Join a Bible study, read a book, find a mentor, take a spiritual retreat, meditate on Scripture, make daily time for God, seek counseling)

7. There is always a spiritual battle trying to pull our hearts away from authenticity. Where are you weak or most vulnerable? What can you do to see victory in that area? Who will help/pray for you? Who will you help/pray for?

The Authentic Musician

4. What's the Point of Music Anyway?

"To everything, turn, turn, turn. There is a season, turn, turn, turn. And a time to every purpose under heaven."... Yes, that's an old '60s song. It's also a true statement from the Old Testament.

Is there a purpose to music? Does God have anything to say about music and the arts? As Christians, we accept that the Bible is our first place to look for direction and perspective on any subject. It dawned on me a while back that I never really researched this topic very thoroughly even though I was deeply involved in producing music. Yet, if we fail to truly understand God's purpose for our art, we've missed too much. Here's what I found.

#1 Music and the Arts Are a Gift

Music has been around for a long time. The Bible speaks of music existing even before man was created. In Job 38:7, God himself says that the stars sang together as the earth was being created. This may be metaphorical, but still it acknowledges that at least the concept of music existed before creation. Even Satan, who existed before man was made, is also thought to have been a musician before falling from his place in heaven (Is 14:11). And we also know that angels, who existed before the Earth's creation, can sing (Rev 5). Plus, even the Earth and heavens are exhorted to sing (Is 44)! Therefore, we can say that music is not just a creation of man but that it has been created by God and has existed since before the creation of mankind.

The apostle Paul tells us,*"For by him all things were created, in heaven and on earth, visible and invisible, whether thrones or dominions or rulers or authorities—all things were created through him and for him."*[16]

God created music and He delights in it—so much so that music is present in nearly every picture of worship in both the Old and New Testament. From Old Testament Hebrew life to the future heavenly scenes in the book of Revelation, both vocal and instrumental music play a major role in expressing love to God and one another. God clearly delights in music.

Music also is a scientific phenomenon. It has been defined as "organized sound"; that is, it contains pitch, rhythm and timbre (tone). Plus, in different cultures music has been organized into different forms for different purposes. It is interesting that our brains apparently recognize pitch naturally. (See *Your Brain on Music* by Daniel Levitan.) In fact, our ears naturally recognize the 12 half steps of a scale as well as octaves. Of course, not all cultures or styles play off the western diatonic (eight-step) or chromatic (12 half-step) scale, but no music has developed that is built on any other notes than the 12 steps in an octave. Obviously, certain cultures and styles bend notes, but all recognize the fundamental tones of the chromatic scale. God has created our ears to hear music and our brains are "pre-wired" to recognize the pitch differences in a chromatic scale. Amazing!

What's the Point of Music Anyway?

What about other art forms?

Music is the predominant art form used in Bible times. Other art forms are also gifts from God. There are examples and allusions to other forms of art, especially in Old Testament temple life, such as drawing, sculpting, dance and drama (storytelling). However, some forms simply had not evolved when the Bible was written. Obviously God did not create cinema but allowed and perhaps even inspired its creators. Regardless, all of these creative expressions are intended to be used under the umbrella of God's purposes.

Five categories of the arts:

Music – the art of combining rhythm, melody, harmony and lyrics (sometimes) to produce live or recorded music that either informs, entertains or moves people emotionally or spiritually.

Drama – the art of combining a script, cast, set and blocking, choreography, staging, etc., to produce dramatic presentations that entertain, inform or move people emotionally or spiritually.

Dance – the art of combining music (usually), dancers and choreography to create productions that move people emotionally or spiritually.

Visual arts – drawing, painting, sculpting, constructing or producing photography that engages people visually to entertain or move them.

Electronic Visual arts – that art of combining drama, music and photography or cinematography and direction to produce film or video that either entertains, informs or moves people emotionally or spiritually.

#2 Music and the Arts are Valuable

God not only created music and the arts, but He also affirms the use of the arts in human life. The first musician is mentioned in the book of Genesis: *"Jubal; he was the father of all those who play the lyre and pipe."*[17]

The Authentic Musician

Later, in Exodus, God instructed Moses and certain people were commissioned to creatively embellish the tabernacle. *The Lord said to Moses, "See, I have called by name Bezalel the son of Uri, son of Hur, of the tribe of Judah, and I have filled him with the Spirit of God, with ability and intelligence, with knowledge and all craftsmanship, to devise artistic designs, to work in gold, silver, and bronze, in cutting stones for setting, and in carving wood, to work in every craft. And behold, I have appointed with him Oholiab... And I have given to all able men ability, that they may make all that I have commanded you..." (Ex 31:1-6).*

In fact, God designated a whole tribe of Israel, the Levites, for the work of the tabernacle offerings and feasts. *"At that time the LORD set apart the tribe of Levi to carry the ark of the covenant of the LORD to stand before the LORD to minister to him and to bless in his name, to this day."*[18]

And some of the Levites were later called to be musicians and singers. *"And the Levites carried the ark of God on their shoulders with the poles, as Moses had commanded according to the word of the LORD. David also commanded the chiefs of the Levites to appoint their brothers as the singers who should play loudly on musical instruments, on harps and lyres and cymbals, to rise with sounds of joy"*[19] and later: *"Then he (David) appointed some of the Levites as ministers before the ark of the LORD, to invoke, to thank, and to praise the LORD, the God of Israel. Asaph was the chief, and second to him were Zechariah, Jeiel, Shemiramoth, Jehiel, Mattithiah, Eliab, Benaiah, Obed-edom, and Jeiel, who were to play harps and lyres; Asaph was to sound the cymbals, and Benaiah and Jahaziel the priests were to blow trumpets regularly before the ark of the covenant of God."*[20] God's art!

In the book of Deuteronomy even before the tabernacle instructions, God taught a song to Moses, which he was to teach the people of Israel warning them of their waywardness and reminding them of His goodness (Deut 31:17). He surely had a purpose for this song.

God also gave Moses meticulous instructions concerning the building of the tabernacle, including what colors were to be used and what the artwork should look like. He instructed Moses to find people whom He had gifted to construct the tabernacle and do the intricate artwork (weaving, metal sculpture, sewing, etc.). At one point He even states that things were to be created not only for glory (bringing attention to God) or function, but also just for *beauty* (Ex 28:2,40). More could be written about this, but the point here is to remember that not all art has to have a utilitarian purpose. (See *Art and the Bible* by Francis Schaeffer.)

Art Has Value

- Art has value because man as a creator is a reflection of God the Creator.
- Art has value because it can touch people with truth, give encouragement, warning, and comfort, etc.
- Art has value because it serves as a form of expression for the artist. The psalms are a great example.
- Art has value because God delights in it when it glorifies Him. It is present in nearly every one of the scenes of worship in heaven.

Colossians 1:16 reminds us that music was not only created by God but *for* Him. In Romans 11 Paul says, "from him and through him and *to him* are all things. To him be glory forever. Amen." And 1 Corinthians 10 says, "Whatever you do, do all *to the glory of God.*"

We are called to glorify God in every circumstance and with everything. We were created for this purpose and we find our greatest fulfillment in doing so. What does "glorify God" mean? Webster says it means to make glorious by bestowing honor, praise, or admiration.[21] This doesn't mean that every word or lyric or drawing should be about God, but that our inner lives and relationships should reflect the life God intended. It means that our worldview as a Christian should come through our art. (See Schaeffer, *Art and the Bible.*) Remember too that the Bible does not separate the sacred and the secular. We can glorify God everywhere we walk, in our mundane actions and in how we treat others, as much as we can by going to church on Sunday. We are called to live lives set apart to God in all areas, even our thoughts (2 Cor 10:6).

Another way to put this is to say that we should *magnify* God with our lives and abilities. Not like a microscope, which makes an image look bigger than it actually is.... More like a telescope, which "brings into view" that which appears small or even non-existent to the naked eye, but in reality is really big![22] Art has the amazing potential to "bring into view" in a relevant and unique way the heart of God and the truth He has revealed, as well as the artist's heart and worldview. The arts have the power to enhance celebration, amplify reflection and illumine introspection. Art is valuable!

Again, lest you think this means we should spend all of our time in church, singing religious music or doing "sacred" things, remember that God created all of life. Jesus lived a fully devoted life in every aspect, perfectly. He created the Earth and sky, animals, space, the human mind, body and emotions. He is well aware of our fallen world circumstances. In the midst of this He has called us to live a Christ-like life in all ways and to use the arts as a means of expression. Jesus had strong words for people who didn't allow God in to every area of their lives; he called them hypocrites. How we live in relationship with others, how we approach difficulties, our character, how we spend our time, energy and money--all are to glorify God by showing His love, His joy, His power, His peace and His Kingship in our lives by word and action. No small order!

What's the Point of Music Anyway?

A Warning

There are times in the Bible as well when God condemns the wrongful use of the arts. For example, in the book Amos, God says, "Woe to those who are at ease in Zion, ...who sing idle songs to the sound of the harp and like David invent for themselves instruments of music...but are not grieved over the ruin of Joseph (Israel)."

Is Music Amoral?

Music itself is actually just a series of sound waves that enter our ears and go into our brains. So yes, music (sound) is amoral, however, as our brains receive the sound from our ears or an image from our eyes, our mind makes associations with not only the sound or colors but also the words or content. So then, while the sound or colors themselves are amoral, the lyric or content of a piece itself has moral value. Our minds associate previous experiences and perceptions with the words and style. It may associate good or bad things, and it is up to our conscience to determine if this is good or bad for us. For some people the associations with certain styles of music or art are unhealthy or painful for them. Let me explain.

Because of a previous bad experience you may associate with a particular song or form of artistic expression, your mind and heart may conjure up things that become temptations to meditate on, or worse, to sin upon. When this happens, you should stop and turn from that music or art. Turn it off, change the station, walk away from it. This line of association is flexible, however. As we grow and renew our hearts, it is possible to disassociate the negative things and begin to appreciate the style or form of art, without the overwhelming temptations to sin. It is also important to ask God to heal you of the painful associations you have and to bring to your heart the good associations with a particular style of music or art. You must always be careful though (1 Cor10:12). You must also be careful not to impose your boundaries on others, but without casting judgment encourage them to pursue a clear conscience. Because music or artistic styles are amoral, they can be treated much like the meat offerings mentioned in Romans 14. Believers were not to partake of meat offered to idols if they knew it would violate another believer's conscience. Similarly, we must not lead another toward a compromise in their walk with God.

Please note that I am saying that the lyrics or message of a song or work of art *do* present moral values. Lyrics or images that are clearly sinful or dishonoring to God and His word should be discarded. Sad to say, there is a lot of it out there ... songs with profanity, art that is basically pornographic, etc. The only reason a believer should give this "art" any consideration is to perhaps understand the deeper message of where non-believers are coming from—in order to understand our culture and to reach people for Christ. But, this should be done with accountability or in community, and with great vigilance over your own heart.

The principle here is to not violate your conscience or walk into an environment you know will have temptations too strong for you. As you grow stronger, though, it may be that your conscience will allow you to appreciate or even enjoy a style of music or art without the negative associations.

When I was playing in a rock band, I got into conversations with pastors or young Christians about the styles of music we played or artists we covered. On occasion these guys told me when we played Beach Boys music, for example, that all it brought up in their minds were memories of getting drunk and having sex. For them and where they were in their lives, they could not get past these associations and just have fun enjoying the music (the lyrics were good). They needed to walk away from our concert. These same people, months or years later, were able to enjoy the music and see the relevance of using it to build a bridge to non-believers.

What's the Point of Music Anyway?

How then should we evaluate art?

All art carries a message, even if the artist isn't intending to convey a message; his "non-message" is his message. It's the content or message, whether lyrical or emotional (through our associations), that influences us and is important. And it's the message of the art we receive —either its message or our interpretation—that gives it moral impact. This brings us to the value of truth in our art. That which is authentically truthful (from the heart) and influences us toward God's truth is good. That which is inauthentic (dishonest) and has an evil or untrue message is ultimately bad for us. It is possible, however, to use "bad art" for good purposes, e.g.,. to show an audience the need or "lostness" of modern thinking.

I appreciate Francis Schaeffer's suggestion that we evaluate art based on these factors:

1. Technical excellence
2. Validity – whether an artist is honest with himself and to his worldview or whether he makes his art only for money or for the sake of being accepted.
3. Content – that which reflects the world view of the artist
4. Suiting of form and content – the greatest art fits the vehicle being used to the worldview being presented. This is seen in how an artist may have altered a form to emphasize his message, e.g., Picasso's *Demoi-selles d'Avignon* and how he distorted women's faces, etc., to convey the despair of modern life. Often this type of art resulted in great innovation.[23]

Besides the message, music or art also has its own style. How certain styles influence us is very individual and subjective. Truth never changes nor should it be compromised, but different stylistic preferences are very cultural, individual and subjective. You can have the same message put to different musical styles or art forms and get very different reactions from people. For some, one particular style may be very "hip" and to another very offensive. Ultimately our conscience must dictate what we personally like or dislike, without judging another's preference. As artists, we must work out our own approach to handling these differences. As I've mentioned before, God has created the arts to impact us in ways that transcend what just spoken or written words usually do.

Remember too that our art, music or craft should not be valued above our relationship with God and other people. This is a dead-end, unfulfilling road. We should not expect our art or music to deliver more in our lives than it actually can, nor should we minimize the gift that it is. Our fallen world is prone to distort the value of the arts in one direction or the other. Throughout history, there have been times when we have relegated the arts to the fringe of life or at other times, to the very center of life. We must be careful to seek and remember God's perspective if we're going to use and enjoy these gifts to their fullest.

Okay, so far it's clear that the arts are a gift and a valuable means of expression. But for whom and why?

#3 Music and the Arts Are for the Expression of our Hearts

For many of us, it was the desire to express our heart—emotions, dreams, and thoughts—that led us to get seriously involved in the arts in the first place. Expressing ourselves artistically is very often therapeutic. It also can encourage others and give people a window into our soul. It is clearly a gift, though at times you may feel it is a burden!

King David used his poetic and musical gifts often to express his heart to God. The Old Testament book of Psalms is filled with his creations. *"And David spoke to the LORD the words of this song on the day when the LORD delivered him from the hand of all his enemies, and from the hand of Saul"* [24]

What's the Point of Music Anyway?

History, both biblical and otherwise, is filled with artistic expression. Some of it is truly "from the heart;" some is also clearly simply utilitarian. (Muzac anyone?) Is there a place for "utilitarian art" or "community art"? Yes, here again we see examples of songs for the community of Israel given by God and songs that helped served purposes other than self-expression.

As an artist, what should your perspective be on your art? Francis Schaeffer also offers these thoughts:

"There are, I believe three basic possibilities concerning the nature of a work of art. The first view is the relatively recent theory of art for art's sake. This is the notion that art is just there and that is all there is to it. You can't talk about it, you can't analyze it, and it doesn't say anything. This view is, I think, quite misguided. The great modern artists such as Picasso never worked for only art for art's sake either. Picasso has a philosophy that showed through in his paintings.

The second, which I spoke of above, is that art is only an embodiment of a message, a vehicle for prorogation of a particular message about the world or the artist or man or whatever. Christians as well as non-Christians have held this view, the difference between the two versions being the nature of the message that the art embodies. But, as I have said, this view reduces art to an intellectual statement and the work of art as a work of art disappears.

The third basic notion of the nature of art—the one that I think is right, the one that really produces great art and the possibility of great art— is that the artist makes a body of work and this body of work shows his world view... I emphasize the body of an artist's work because it is impossible for any single painting, for example, to reflect the totality of an artist's view of reality. But when we see a collection of an artist's paintings or a series of a poet's poems or a number of a novelist's novels, both the outline and some of the details of the artist's conception of life shine through." [25]

An authentic artist is free to express his heart. Christians should seek to utilize their gifts to the fullest because of this freedom and the connection they have with the Creator himself! And ultimately, just as God creates beauty and displays truth through His creation, so also our life work of art should reveal truth and beauty.

An Artist's Values

Understanding that you have a new heart in Christ can not only free you to express your heart, but it can also affect the process of how and what you create. In other words, certain values accompany a renewed mind and heart. Here are just a few points to ponder.

Excellence vs. Perfectionism

Any serious artist has to face her performance level regularly. Typically we fall into the category of "perfectionist" rather than a "pursuer of excellence." There is a difference. In fact, in education settings, very often perfection is rewarded more than excellence. Perfection is the belief that there is a perfect way to do something and that my self-worth is tied to my performance or others' opinions. If I don't play something "perfectly" or create the perfect sculpture, etc., I am a failure. Often it is the need for others' acceptance, our own pride or our woundedness that drives this unhealthy compulsion. This often leaves a trail of violated relationships and depression in its wake as well. Perfectionism has served as a powerful motivation for many artists and has led to some amazing works of art for sure. However, if we understood the real nature of our call to excellence we would leave this lesser motivation in the dust.

What's the Point of Music Anyway?

Excellence is the pursuit of doing our very best with our gifts while drawing our self-worth from who God says we are and not from our performance or others' opinions. Excellence flows from realizing we have been freed from the kingdom of darkness to the kingdom of light— freed to bring pleasure to the awesome God of the universe through our gifts! The drive in this case is love—loving God and loving our neighbor as ourselves. Does this mean we don't try to do something "perfectly"? Absolutely not! It means we should evaluate our performance by asking if we gave our best effort. Perfectionism is a striving with unhealthy motives; excellence is an attitude that pushes us to do even better next time. Perfection looks to our achievement for fulfillment; excellence looks to our identity in Christ for fulfillment. Perfection defines success by creating the perfect "product" at all costs. Excellence defines success by having an excellent product and process from start to finish.

Excellence is a value authentic musicians should carry with them always. Is it easy? No. Do we ever fail at it? Yes. It is an attitude we must cultivate in all we do. *"Whatever you do, work heartily, as for the Lord and not for men, knowing that from the Lord you will receive the inheritance as your reward. You are serving the Lord Christ" (Col 3:23).*

Creativity vs. Replication

God created the universe we live in, from the biggest star to the smallest molecule. One look at creation—the variety, the beauty, the intricacy, the uniqueness—and we see it explodes with creativity every day! Man, being created in God's image, has also been given the ability to create not out of nothing, like God, but out of matter. We discover and reshape, develop and produce all manner of things.

Some pitfalls with creativity are that very often the creative process is either never fully pursued due to a lack of time, resources and energy, or creativity is pursued without any accountability or evaluation.

73

The Authentic Musician

Our society of instant gratification often simply settles for replication rather than innovation. It's easier and takes less energy and resources. If an immediate, measurable profit is not realized then it is abandoned. This is not to say there should never be measurable, monetary results, but when the utilitarian purpose is *all* we look for (or an organization looks for), creativity will be squelched. We settle for mediocre achievements due to our own indifference.. It's worth noting too that history has shown how much a culture's worldview and values have affected an artist's creativity. For example, the reformation and counter-reformation eras of history had a huge impact on creativity and artistic expression in Europe, as did the Dark Ages.

So where is the balance? How do we maintain a creative edge in our art? I believe God is our model in this. He created. He saw. He declared. He rested.

Others have put it in terms of:

- Idea
- Incubation
- Implementation
- Evaluation
- Celebration

Realize that there is a *rhythm* to the creative process. The amount of time needed in each stage depends on the scope of the creation, your capacity as an artist and the resources available to you.

Other valuable elements are accountability and teamwork. Many artists resist accountability. It's too confining or takes too much time. But, one look at anyone who has accomplished much creatively will reveal a whole host of teachers, mentors and friends who've been there to encourage, give feedback and also connect the artist with reality (☺). Now, admittedly, many times teamwork and creativity don't work well for an artist. Often the creative process involves considerable times of

74

solitude and there's nothing wrong with this. At the same time, though, there is a proper time to bring in a team to help with a project or give feedback. Some projects really work better in the context of a team, and it can be more fun!

As I mentioned earlier, our culture and we sometimes don't respect this process, and in the end there is a price to pay. Because we live in a fallen world, the creative capacity of man is also diminished. As great as man's creativity has been throughout history, we haven't begun to realize the degree of creativity that will be unleashed when we are in heaven! Nonetheless, we should keep growing in our reflection of this attribute of God now.

Authenticity

This value more than anything can impact those around us. It is what allows us to be humble and teachable as well as to have encouraging relationships in the process. While some in our audiences may not necessarily see our authenticity through our art, most people do sense it and are drawn to it. Authenticity can be inspirational and influential. Combined with well developed gifts, it allows you to speak into other's lives in profound ways.

Other Values

You may identify other values you feel strongly about as you continue to grow. Two other values I always seek to implement in most of my endeavors are community and relevance. Community means I pursue God-honoring relationships in the process. Relevance means I seek to serve my audience in their language as much as possible. These also help me keep on God's agenda for my life.

#4 Music and the Arts Are for the Encouragement of Others

Lifting others up through our art can be extremely gratifying and significant. But so often our reasons for using our gifts are just to express ourselves or to draw attention to ourselves. Helping or encouraging others is easily a lower priority. Such a "me-centered" approach to our art can easily stunt our growth and limit our joy. God has bigger plans for your art. Being truly authentic means being free to express our heart through our creative gifts, of love for God, others and ourselves.

"So, no matter what I say, what I believe, and what I do, I'm bankrupt without love." - from the apostle Paul

To always express our gifts in love is a tall order. In this passage from the New Testament, the apostle Paul goes on to define what love looks like in his own creative prose:

Love never gives up.
Love cares more for others than for self.
Love doesn't want what it doesn't have.
Love doesn't strut,
Doesn't have a swelled head,
Doesn't force itself on others,
Isn't always "me first,"
Doesn't fly off the handle,
Doesn't keep score of the sins of others,
Doesn't revel when others grovel,
Takes pleasure in the flowering of truth,
Puts up with anything,
Trusts God always,
Always looks for the best,

What's the Point of Music Anyway?

Never looks back,

But keeps going to the end.

Love never dies.

(1 Cor 13:1-8, The Message)

How does this definition of love impact your music or art? How would it change your relationships? Your life? Again, it's a tall order, but it's also the kind of love God is working to develop in us because this is His kind of love. He lived it and demonstrated it, and still has this kind of love for each of us.

If we're living by this kind of love, we need only think about the needs of others for the motivation to use our gifts. The arts have a special ability to speak to another's mind, emotions and will. They can help break down emotional barriers, give comfort, refresh and renew people's minds and hearts. The arts can point people to truth and help them identify feelings they may not have even identified yet themselves.

This doesn't mean it's wrong to write a song or create a drawing just as a form of self expression. But if this is the only reason you use your gifts, you are missing a huge part of the reason God has gifted you and a great source of fulfillment. I think most artistic works have a combination of self and others focus.

Paul also reminds us, *"Let each of you look not only to his own interests, but also to the interest of others" (Rmn15:2).*

The Old Testament also encourages us to use our gifts to build up others:

Praise the Lord! Sing to the Lord a new song, his praise in the assembly of the godly! Let Israel be glad in his Maker; let the children of Zion rejoice in their King! Let them praise his name with dancing, making melody to him with tambourine and lyre! For the Lord takes pleasure in his people; he adorns the humble with salvation. (Ps 149:1-3)

Also:

He put a new song in my mouth, a song of praise to our God.

Many will see and fear, and put their trust in the Lord. (Ps40:3)

Your music or art can greatly encourage people emotionally. It can help people think differently or change their attitude. It can also help to move people spiritually. This is a big part of the reason God has blessed you with artistic gifts. He called people in the Old Testament and still today calls us to use our gifts to help others find eternal life and grow in their worship of Him.

I was blown away after playing some of my own music for a Christian outreach event when I was 19. After realizing God used me and our music to help others to accept Christ as their Savior, I was awestruck. I had discovered a higher purpose for developing and using my gifts. To think that God could use me and my abilities to help someone come to know Him personally and have eternal life was incredible! Until that point, music was mostly a means of gaining others' acceptance or for self-gratification. But to think I could use it to help move people spiritually, for *their* eternal good, was amazing! More on that later...

#5 Music and the Arts Are for the Pleasure of God

Send out your light and your truth; let them lead me;
Let them bring me to your holy hill and to your dwelling!
Then I will go to the alter of God, to God my exceeding joy,
And I will praise you with the lyre, O God, my God. (Ps43:3,4)

Have you ever thought about having God as your audience? It's an awesome thought, quite humbling and amazing. David is clearly expressing his heart here in this passage. His intimate one-on-one relationship with God is his inspiration and he can't help but use his music to worship God.

Elsewhere David says, *"He lifted me up on a rock, making my footsteps firm and he put a new song in my mouth, a hymn of praise to my God, many will see and fear...*(Ps 40:3). Here David says that God even gave him a song of praise.

Author Rick Warren puts it this way: "You were planned for God's pleasure. The moment you were born into the world, God was there as an unseen witness, smiling at your birth. He wanted you alive, and your arrival gave him great pleasure. God did not need to create you, but he chose to create you for his own enjoyment. You exist for his benefit, his glory, his purpose and his delight. Bringing enjoyment to God, living for his pleasure, is the first purpose of your life."

He continues: "Bringing pleasure to God is called worship. The Bible says, 'The Lord is pleased with those who worship him and trust his love' (Ps 147:11, CEV). Anything you do that brings pleasure to God is an act of worship. Like a diamond, worship is multifaceted. Anthropologists have noted that worship is a universal urge, hard-wired by God into the very fiber of our being—an inbuilt need to connect with God." [26]

I want to be careful to emphasize that God ultimately looks at our heart, not just our music. But if our hearts are fully His in worship, then He also delights in the expression of our love for Him through our art or music.

As Christians, the "Audience of One" is with us always (Heb13:5). The Psalms and numerous other passages serve as huge evidence of God's delight when authentic artists express their love, praise and adoration to Him. Our experience of God's presence and power through our obedience can serve as a great motivation to use our gifts. This is clearly seen in many passages of Scripture. For example, after the nation of Israel experienced God's power and deliverance from the Egyptians and the Red Sea, they broke out into song and dance. They could not help but praise Him. Many of King David's songs came out of direct experiences with God. As you read some of his Psalms, it's almost as if he experiences God as he writes and his heart is changed in the process. As people experienced Jesus' healing presence in the New Testament, often the response was simply to worship Him. And the book of Revelation clearly shows us responsive songs of worship at the revelation of the Lamb of God.

And when he had taken the scoll, the four living creatures and the twenty-four elders fell down before the Lamb, each holding a harp, and golden bowls full of incense, which are the prayers of the saints. And they sang a new song. (Rev5:8,9)

God delights in this kind of worship. He created us for this purpose and He is worthy of our worship. Is it egotistical of God to delight in worship of Himself? Not if He is worthy of it!

John Piper's book, *Let the Nations Be Glad*, reminds us that "God is most glorified in us when we are most satisfied in him... if it is true, then it becomes plain why God is loving when he seeks to exalt his glory in my life, for that would mean that he would seek to maximize my satisfaction in him, since he is most glorified in me when I am most satisfied in him. Therefore, God's pursuit of his own glory is not at odds with my joy, and that means it is not unkind or unmerciful or unloving of him to seek his glory. In fact, it means that the more passionate God is for his own glory, the more passionate he is for my satisfaction in that glory. And therefore, God's God-centeredness and God's love soar together."[27]

The old story is told of two stonemasons working on a great church in Europe. A man came by and asked the first mason, "What are you doing?"

He answered, "Oh, I'm just laying bricks on this mortar to make a wall."

What's the Point of Music Anyway?

He came upon another mason and asked him, "What are you doing?"

This mason replied, "I'm building a great church to the glory of God!"

What was the difference? One saw God as his audience and the other didn't. Realizing we have God as our audience and that we can glorify Him with our gifts can serve as our greatest motivation in life. This is especially true in your times alone. Artists usually spend a lot of time alone crafting their skills or art, and it can be very discouraging to continue trying ideas that don't work or fail to "produce" as we would like. On the other hand, it is incredibly motivating to know God's presence in these times. To know that He sees and hears, and delights in our offerings even from a practice room is incredible! He desires to be at the heart of our creative process as well as the end product. Of course, part of the key to experiencing this type of intimacy with God is our obedience to Him. When we allow unrepentant sin in our lives, our intimacy with God suffers If, however, we're walking in His light, even practicing in a desolate practice room can be an act of worship! Knowing Him as our first love is incredibly humbling and motivating.

So why should we be excited about music and the arts? *Music and the arts are valuable gifts from God, for the expression of our hearts, the encouragement of others and the pleasure of God.*

I encourage you to meditate on the above statement and see if this changes how you approach your creative gifts. How would our world be different if we artists fully applied God's calling and purposes for our gifts?

Follow-up Questions

Chapter 4: What's the point of music anyway?

1. What was your view of music before reading this chapter? How has it changed?

2. *The arts are a valuable gift from God for the expression of our hearts.* Do you agree with that statement? How much do you express your heart through your art? Is it a priority for you to engage your heart in your music/art?

3. What values do you try to uphold in your art? Where do they come from?

4. *The arts are a valuable gift from God... for the encouragement of others.* Is this a motivating factor in your art? How do you encourage others by using your gifts?

5. *The arts are a valuable gift from God... for the pleasure of God.* J.S. Bach signed many of his original scores with the initials S.D.G. (Soli Deo Gloria), "To God Alone, Glory." Is the idea of worshipping God through your art foreign to you? Why or why not?

5. Relating to Other Artists: Comparing, Competing and Contributing

"Teamwork makes the dream work." (John Maxwell)

How do you relate to other artists? Are you threatened by them? Are you inspired by them? Are you depressed by them? Should you care at all?

If you've had formal music or artistic education, from the beginning you entered into a world of comparing and eventually competing to prove as well as improve your skills. In fact, the whole process of learning to play an instrument, paint or sculpt usually occurs through a mentor or teacher who instructs as well as provides examples (either in their own playing or others) for you to compare your work with. This is meant to be inspiring and often provides great insight into our own improvement as long as we can see how to get from A to B or E or M. Our public education system also is built on the value of comparison and competition, not only in the arts and sports but also many other disciplines. And it has been quite effective. The drive to "beat" another person or team is a powerful motivator, and our culture makes heroes of those who are "winners." Winning and losing can be powerful motivators to grow and excel.

The Authentic Musician

I remember my own competitions with other trumpet players in junior high and high school. We regularly competed for first chair, and I have to admit that in my situation it wasn't always very motivating. If I won, of course I felt great about myself and felt I deserved some applause. But if I lost, I often felt I was somehow a failure—personally. For those who weren't first chair, it was easy to feel inferior to the "big guys" and even easier for the "big guys" to flaunt their position—not a real healthy or enjoyable environment for everyone in the band.

While I'm not against competitiveness in the arts, I believe there is a danger in a wrong approach to it. When we begin to draw our self-worth and self-esteem from our position or performance, problems arise. While competing, you may find yourself wishing your competition would fail miserably. When you win, you might gloat in your superiority and demand respect from other people. This can lead to a "prima donna" complex or egotistical attitude, either of which does nothing positive for your relationships. When you lose, it *can* be devastating to your self-worth and lead to many negative reactions....allowing "revenge" to be your motivation,   crying foul and playing the victim of injustice, or allowing depression and hopelessness about your playing or even yourself to take over.

While it's not intrinsically bad to compare yourself with others or to compete for the top place, when we make our position a measure of our self-worth or self-esteem, it becomes destructive. One of the earliest stories in the Bible illustrates the danger of unhealthy comparison and competition. Cane and Able were told to give an offering to the Lord and for Cain this became a competition and test of self-worth.

Cain was unable to handle God's acceptance of Able's offering and rejection of his. His resentment grew to the point of breaking any type of relationship he had with Able. This led to Able's murder, even though God had warned Cain that "sin was crouching at the door."

Relating to Other Artists: Comparing, Competing and Contributing

Author C.S. Lewis wrote in *Mere Christianity*, *"Pride is essentially competitive... Pride gets no pleasure out of having something, only out of having more of it than the next man. We say people are proud of being rich, or clever, or good-looking, but they are not. They are proud of being richer, or cleverer, or better-looking than others."* (Or a better musician than others.)

A handy saying that emerges from this type of insecure comparison looks like this: *Unhealthy comparison leads to unhealthy competition, which kills community.*

On the other hand, I would propose that *healthy comparison can lead to healthy competition, which leads to healthy contribution, which builds community (and a successful production)!* There is a better and higher way than just competing, which I believe an authentic artist should aspire to.

Comparison

All of us know the negative or positive feelings we get when we hear a superior musician, especially if they play our instrument. Either it's discouraging: "It's useless, why try?" Or it's inspiring: "Wow, I want to learn to do what she did!"

Comparing yourself with others is an important way to learn. It's the way we *respond* to comparison that makes all the difference. In fact, as artists we should always be seeking to learn from other more advanced artists. You won't go very far unless you are willing to compare your playing with more advanced players. And when you remove the ego aspect, this actually makes the process much more fun and fruitful! You can learn to appreciate other artists without being threatened and find great encouragement when they reciprocate respect and interest.

Healthy comparison is valuable in other areas of life, too. On the spiritual side, the apostle Paul boldly encouraged early believers to learn from his example: "Follow me as I follow Christ." He is urging comparison. As well, we should often compare our way with the way of Christ if we're going to grow spiritually. The traditional Christian season of Lent often focuses on this.

Competition

Competition can be a healthy motivator when you remove the "self-significance" element from it. To do this, though, you must have a good context or reason for your competition. The context might simply be *self-improvement*—yours and the other person's. Or it could be the team's *improvement* (band, ensemble, choir, artistic community, etc.), with an excellent product or a winning performance as your goal. Excellence is always the best goal for your performance. It simply means you're going to give your absolute best effort throughout your preparation and performance; it is not focused only on results. Just as excellence is the best value to drive competition for the individual, it is also the highest motivation for a team. With the excellence of your team in mind, competition becomes a means of developing the best "product" by having the most skilled players in the right place.

If our hearts are in the right place on this, we will view competition simply as a tool to assess someone's abilities, affirm the best fit for their abilities and the needs of the organization, and help members identify areas they need to grow. It is not an opportunity to dominate someone and proudly gloat, or to be destructively jealous, or to deprecate your own self-worth or self-esteem. It is key to separate your performance from who you are, or someone else's performance from their value as a person.

Relating to Other Artists: Comparing, Competing and Contributing

How you respond when another is promoted above you says a lot about your character. To be jealous is to covet or want something you have no right to and to disregard the person who rightfully has what you want. When this happens, our natural response is jealousy. But the better response is to celebrate another's success. This is not the normal atmosphere of most bands or organizations, and it's a chance to let our light shine. It also frees us to pursue true excellence. Author Andy Stanley writes, *"Celebration is how you defeat jealousy."*

Artists who pursue excellence:
* Always seek to do their *best* with what gifts they have
* Seek to grow and *excel* in their craft by learning from others, practicing, stretching themselves, etc.
* Draw their self-worth from who they are in Christ, not their performance.
* Create their art to glorify God and fulfill His purposes as a steward of the gifts they've been given.

A team that pursues excellence:
* Believes that its combined best efforts accomplish more than individual performances.
* Is driven by worthy team goals and synergy.
* Maintains an attitude of humility and encouragement.
* Always seeks to do its best, excel still more, and is free from personal significance issues.
* Pursues integrity as a team and respects other teams, wishing their best.

The Authentic Musician

From Competitor to Contributor

There is a better paradigm to bring to our teams and relationships with other artists than just being a competitor. If you draw your self-worth from your performance, you will become a competitor only. But if you are living authentically before God, you will approach your team and relationships as a *contributor* who pursues *excellence* for yourself and your team.

A contributor:

- Believes in the team's goals and potential
- Seeks the best for his team and team members
- Encourages others to do their best
- Models excellence to her teammates
- Uses comparison and competition to improve his skills and motivate others to grow.
- Cares about teammates apart from how they perform

Applying It All

So, back to my original questions: How do you relate to other artists? Do they threaten you? Do they inspire you? Do they depress you? Should you care at all?

We all know what the usual artistic culture looks like. So it is up to the authentic artists to raise the bar by their example. This is part of what Jesus meant by saying we are the light of the world and salt of the earth!

Perhaps a better question is, "How *well* are you relating to other artists?" Are you improving as a contributor instead of just a competitor? Are you comparing yourself to other artists with humility and teachability? Are you competing with an attitude of excellence while also desiring the same from your competition?

It gets back to love....An authentic musician relates authentically with others. Ultimately, that means we love others as we are called to

Relating to Other Artists: Comparing, Competing and Contributing

love. And our example is Jesus Christ, the supreme example of excellence in his relationship with the Father and others. He pursued God's best and lived out every aspect of His calling with excellence. He also knew the secret and power of dependence on His Father to accomplish the work. We see this reflected in Jesus' prayer life (Luke 5:16) among other things. Even more so, if you seek to relate authentically to others, you will be driven to prayer for yourself and others as you grow in your love. Funny how when it comes to relationships, it always gets back to love!

Such a relational atmosphere in a group acts as a magnet to others. This is part of God's plan. Whether it's a team, a community, a family or a marriage, when there are authentic, God honoring relationships, there is an attraction and impact on others. We'll explore more on this in Chapter 8 on Authentic Relationships.

And this I pray, that your love may abound still more and more in real knowledge and all discernment, so that you may approve the things that are excellent, in order to be sincere and blameless until the day of Christ; having been filled with the fruit of righteousness which comes through Jesus Christ, to the glory and praise of God (Phil 1:9-11)

Follow-up Questions

Chapter 5: Relating to Other Artists: comparing, competing, and contributing

1. Of the three categories, where do you find yourself most often (comparison, competitor, contributor)? Do you agree that the contributor paradigm is better when it comes to relating to other artists?

2. What can you change about yourself to be a contributor more consistently?

3. How would you define excellence? Is it a high value for you? Why or why not?

4. Are there ways your team (if you're on one) could foster a stronger contributor atmosphere versus a competitor atmosphere?

6. Me? Impact People Through Music?

"The life I touch for good or ill will touch another life, and that in turn another, until who knows where the trembling stops or in what far place my touch will be felt" (Frederick Buechner). [28]

So far we've seen that the arts are valuable gifts from God for the expression of our hearts, the encouragement of others and the pleasure of God. And an authentic artist is someone who knows his giftedness, develops his skill, and creates his art with a "spiritually alive" heart.

It might seem obvious, looking at these definitions, that the authentic expression of our gifts will have an impact on people. But it wasn't until I was in my early twenties that I even began to realize my music was a gift to be expressed for the good of others, not just my own pleasure. I don't think we have to dwell on the fact that our artistic gifts benefit us personally. For most of us, the reason we got involved in the arts to begin with was for our own expression (which is okay) or perhaps for our own acceptance by significant others. To start off, let's answer these questions .

The Authentic Musician

Should We Try to Influence People Through Our Art?

There is a place for heartfelt self-expression and God-adoring worship in our music or art. We miss a lot of our purpose, however, if those are the only uses of our art.

Music and the arts throughout history have been powerful tools that have influenced people and even nations. In biblical history, Israel's songs of victory and lament called them to repent, worship and love. In the early church the use of psalms, hymns and spiritual songs toward one another was actually commanded. In all cultures, music and the arts have had a significant role in shaping people's thinking. Artists from ancient through modern cultures have used their art to try to influence people for good or bad—speaking to both specific individuals and groups. The "revolution songs" of the late '60s are such a clear example of artists using their gifts to try to influence the "establishment" culture. Songwriter Bob Dylan comments on his beliefs about music: "Music can save people, but it can't in the commercial way it's being used. It's just too much. It's pollution." [29]

One author commented on rock music, "Rock's sheer pervasiveness makes it the most profound value shaper in existence today. Unless you are deaf it is virtually guaranteed that rock music has affected your view of the world." [30] (I would say that today's movies are also having an even greater impact on people's worldview.)

On the negative side Vladimir Lenin, the co-founder of communism and one of history's experts on subversion and revolution, said, "One quick way to destroy a society is through its music." [31]

Christian artists such as Larry Norman, Keith Green and even Bob Dylan were unashamedly calling for change in the culture in the '70s and '80s and were met with both rejection and acceptance.

We could also trace other revolutions (American and French, American Civil War) and find great songs of inspiration and exhortation.

Me? Impact People Through Music?

Current examples are U2 and other bands standing behind the One campaign or England's "Red Nose Day" to end global poverty and fight the Aids pandemic. They take up the mantle of declaring the need for change in our wayward, insensitive, consumerist society. (You can probably think of many others.) They and others continue trying to alert us to the threats and devastation we see instantly with our "live" media.

But wait, there's more!

As if the needs of our physical world weren't enough to motivate us, there is also a world *behind* the seen world, which beckons an authentic artist to lift his voice to reach those who desperately need to know the truth of Christ.

The Bible's implications of the spiritual needs of people are enormous. While we see heartbreaking physical needs all around us—enough to totally depress us if we take them all in—it is incredibly humbling, overwhelming and inspiring to realize Jesus has also called us to meet spiritual needs by proclaiming His truth. This is not to say we should ignore the physical needs of people or using the arts to alert people to those needs. In fact, very often the way to meeting people's spiritual needs is through meeting physical needs. But on the other side, we mustn't neglect getting to the ultimate spiritual needs of people around the world: their need to receive Christ personally and begin to experience new life in Him.

If God could use you and your art to help someone else move from inauthenticity to authenticity, from spiritual death to spiritual life, from darkness to light, from eternal separation from God to eternal life, would you want Him to?

While the quick answer to this question may be yes, let us also continually remind ourselves of the significance of having God's answers to people's greatest spiritual needs and His call for us to use our gifts to share those truths in sometimes *sacrificial* ways. Embarking on this type of mission with our music or art will meet resistance from spiritual forces also. Our prayer should be for God to continually open our eyes to the spiritual realities and opportunities around us *as well as* physical needs. It was this passion to "seek and to save lost" for God's glory that drove Jesus' ministry, and as He was sent into the world, so are we. He ministered to physical and spiritual needs. Here was His mission statement:

"The Spirit of the Lord is upon me, because he has anointed me to proclaim good news to the poor. He has sent me to proclaim liberty to the captives and recovery of sight to the blind, to set at liberty those who are oppressed, to proclaim the year of the Lord's favor" (Lk 4:18).

Here is ours:

"As you sent me into the world, so I have sent them into the world" (Jn 17:18).

Defining your message

If you are freed and called to influence others, what should your message be? Beyond some basic boundaries, every artist must ultimately let his conscience and God's Spirit guide him as he creates a work of art. Also, when we talk about evaluating an artist's work, it is important to look at his entire body of work and not just one piece. Francis Schaeffer emphasizes this point in his book *Art and the Bible*:

Christian art is by no means religious art, that is, art that deals with religious themes... Christian art is the expression of the whole life of the whole person who is a Christian... Art is not to be solely a vehicle of some kind of self-conscious evangelism...The Christian is the really free man –

he is free to have imagination. This too is our heritage. The Christian is the one whose imagination should fly beyond the stars.

Authentic art should reflect truth and beauty, and engage our imagination just as God's art in creation does. As for the message it should:

Please God

We should have a clear conscience over what we're saying and why. Ask God to search and change your ambitions where needed.

Influence others positively

Our message should move others toward good and not toward evil. In other words, love!

Be honest

It should reflect what you're going through. It should reflect your heart and your mind, your worldview and your experience; it should reflect truth and how truth is affecting your life. Life is a journey. Our art, if it's authentic, should reflect that we are living in the reality of pain and suffering, darkness and light, pollution and beauty, etc., as well as God's transforming work in our lives. It's especially interesting to see the transformation that took place in artists like Rembrandt or even Bono. Their worldviews went through very real transformations and their work shows it.

Reflect God's heart

Does God have an agenda for the message you bring besides your own self-expression? Yes, He does. The Bible is clear that God's loving heart for people is:

- That they know Him personally through Jesus Christ. Our art can present these truths (the Gospel) in extremely poignant and relevant ways.
- That they grow in their reflection of Christ and worship of Him. Again, your gifts can communicate to others' hearts the truths that can transform them, especially when you are also a living example of that transformation!
- That they would be salt and light in society. The Gospel (good news) is meant to touch the physical world and the spiritual. Clearly God has a heart for all people, rich and poor, joyful and sorrowful. Our art can encourage people, bringing healing and help. It can inform people of oppression and abuse. God's message speaks in all areas of life and so should our works of art.

Much has been written in recent years regarding Christians giving up the arts to the non-God world. Where at one time Christians were the primary innovators, creators and contributors of art to the world stage, in the last century most of the "cutting edge" art has come from those without a Christian worldview. The messages have often been the opposite of God's heart and very depressing, even harmful.

Recently, however, there are examples of Christian artists having greater influence in Western culture. It's not uncommon to see artists expressing themselves on stages of great influence, in film and video. And in many cases, the artistic caliber or level of expertise is significantly closer to "state of the art" than in years past. There is still, however, a long way to go– both in the technical sense and in the "authentic" (Christ-like) sense.

This will always be a battle because there is the unseen world between heaven and hell vying 24/7 for people's hearts and ultimate destinies. However, there is also great opportunity to take up the mantle to "fight the darkness with light" and be a voice to help people know the true God and experience His transforming love in every area of life and society.

Some other voices:

"Those who perceive in themselves this kind of divine spark which is the artistic vocation—as poet, writer, sculptor, architect, musician, actor and so on—feel at the same time the obligation not to waste this talent but to develop it, in order to put it at the service of their neighbor and of humanity as a whole.... (Pope John Paul-II)" [32]

"For a number of years jazz had a tremendous influence on my thoughts about art and life" (Stuart Davis). [33]

"Life obliges me to do something, so I paint" (Rene Magritte). [34]

"The hallmark of courage in our age of conformity is the capacity to stand on one's own convictions" (Rollo May).[35]

"Where the spirit does not work with the hand there is no art" (Leonardo da Vinci). [36]

What About Persuasion?

Perhaps the question remains—Should we try to move or *persuade* our audience? Why even think about it? Shouldn't we just do our thing and expect the audience to like it or not and leave it at that? It's one thing to just do our music and hope it inspires people; it's another thing, however, to proactively plan and seek to help people change their minds. Caution: I'm not talking about manipulating our audience but rather serving them, to help them see a better way for their lives. Manipulation involves deceptively trying to get something from my audience. Persuasion means I'm honestly seeking to serve my audience for their good. Often this may require personal sacrifice rather than personal benefit.

This persuasion could range from simply trying to move people emotionally to actually persuading people to change their lives. If our goal is love—in the Scriptural sense—then we have a green light from God to do it.

Actually artists have tried for centuries to influence and persuade people through their art; some toward very good ideals and others toward very destructive ideals... some with very selfish motives, others out of love.

In his book, *How Should We Then Live*, Francis Schaeffer made this interesting comment about 20th century art, and for today's culture I believe it is only amplified. He says, "The important concepts of philosophy increasingly began to come not as formal statements of philosophy but rather as expressions in art, music, poetry, drama, and the cinema...Especially in the sixties the major philosophic statements which received a wide hearing were made through films." As the discussion continues, it becomes apparent that artists (of all art forms) not only influence our society, but also should take seriously their role of influencing and persuading society toward righteousness (right living). This is part of what Jesus meant when said his followers are to be salt and light in the world!

Should persuasion be our goal? Should we actually seek to change people's minds? The answer is yes. Persuasion was clearly the goal in the apostle Paul's preaching: "Therefore, knowing the fear of the Lord, we persuade others" (2 Cor 5:11). This wasn't without parameters, however. Notice his first condition "knowing the fear of the Lord." An application of fearing the Lord in this case means we speak the truth in love (Eph 4:15). Another would be to walk in the light throughout your process (1Jn1:7). There are many good books on this subject (see appendix) but I will just touch on a few key points I hope will help. Also, please note that these points are not just for musicians! These principles apply to any form of communication or artistic craft.

Marks of Authentic Persuasion

1. Cultural Relevance

Obviously, Jesus was a great communicator and persuader. He intended always to seek the good of his listeners, even when they rejected Him. He was the most "authentic" communicator ever and He also clearly sought to be culturally relevant. He accomplished this by how He taught and by the very fact that he became a human. Here's how:

Jesus' Teaching Style

When He taught, he used common, everyday pictures and stories to illustrate spiritual truths. His stories and parables centered on people and things His audience could understand and relate to, plus He spoke with authority and conviction. Their response shows they were moved. After teaching on the sermon on the mount, Matthew says, "And when Jesus finished these sayings, the crowds were astonished at his teaching, for he was teaching them as one who had authority, and not as their scribes"(Mt 7:28).

Jesus' Miracles

Obviously Jesus' miracles built credibility with the people. His miracles validated His message and deity. But notice that Jesus could have used signs in the skies or just shown his glory (like the transfiguration), but he choose to deal with people's real needs. The blind beggar, the lame, the grieving mother, the wedding wine—all were very personal, real needs He met that opened the door for more conversation or teaching. It is no different for us! While we may not do miracles, our good works do open doors and they may seem like a miracle to someone. In the words of my pastor, "Good works promote good will which promote good words."

Jesus' Incarnation

It is mind boggling to consider the implications of Jesus' incarnation (God becoming a man). Philippians Chapter 2 reveals to us that Jesus was in the place of ultimate satisfaction and fulfillment with the Father and the Spirit. He was enjoying all of the delight of being with the trinity and of being God, and yet He gave up or emptied Himself of his rights as God to become one of us. Then to come to Earth and live as a perfect man so He could reach us, teach us, and save us is amazing. He could have chosen many other ways to communicate to us but He chose to come into the filth of a sinful human existence, which must have been much more disdainful then we can fathom. He then taught and lived among a dull and rebellious people and continued in His unconditional love to relate to us, ultimately taking upon himself the Father's wrath that we deserved. He died, was crucified and buried, and rose in a new human body that we might still even touch His scarred hands, side and feet, and know His passionate, intimate, long-suffering love. He sought every means possible to demonstrate His love in the most holy and pure yet culturally relevant and effective way. I'm struck especially with the tenacity, passion, patience and long-suffering love of our Savior.

Am I letting the Savior's love drive what I do to reach people on their level? Am I ready and willing to empty myself for the benefit of others?

Paul's Example

The apostle Paul stated clearly in his letters that the goal of his teaching and ministry was to persuade people to accept and follow Christ for God's glory. "Therefore, knowing the fear of the Lord, we persuade others" (2 Cor 5:11). His experience and passion for God fueled his persuasive endeavors, and he even felt that people's eternal destiny was at stake and dependent upon someone persuading them to accept Christ. This was also God's plan when He gave the great commission (Matt 28:18-20, Rom 10:14,15). 1 Corinthians 9:19 states, "For though I am free from all, I have made myself a servant to all, that I might win more of them." Again, Verse 23: "I do it all for the sake of the gospel, that I may share with them in its blessings."

This passage goes on to explain that Paul was willing to become like a Jew, Gentile or whatever, that he might persuade them to follow Christ. "I have become all things to all men, so that I may by all means save some" (1 Cor 9:22). At the same time this never meant compromising the message or his conscience for the sake of persuasion: "For our boast is this: the testimony of our conscience that we behaved in the world with simplicity and godly sincerity, not by earthly wisdom but by the grace of God, and supremely so toward you" (2 Cor 1:12).

2. Sharing the Truth in Love

It is clear in 1 Corinthians 13 that any type of activity, including persuasion, without love as the primary motive is worthless—only a noisy gong or clanging cymbal. When people sense Christlike love, they are touched. They may not know what it is, but they know it's something they need if their hearts are soft.... (2 Cor 2:14-16). Likewise, because God exists and has communicated truth to us, we are obliged to share the truth with others. Jesus said we shall know the truth and the truth shall set us free. It is certainly unloving to withhold the truth from others. In fact, Christ's love in us compels us to share truth with others (2 Cor 5:14). There is no doubt that being culturally relevant with godly love is part of God's plan to reach people.

Audience-Centered Communication

There is, however, a tension when it comes to communication. On one side is the presenter (artist) who needs to operate within her abilities and conscience. On the other side is the listener, who has been preprogrammed to interpret our communication in certain ways, which may or may not be understood or accepted.

Audience-centered communicators maintain their integrity and do all in their power to understand their listeners and relate their message in the most effective way. How is this done? Authentic communicators have the right *attitude* toward their audience, they're *attentive* to their audience's expectations and needs, and they *actively engage* their audience with their story and God's story.

Servant Attitude

The Bible calls us to be both a *steward* of our gifts and of the message, as well a *servant* to our audience. Paul's attitude is clear: *"For we do not preach ourselves, but Jesus Christ as Lord, and ourselves as your servants for Jesus' sake. For God, who said, 'Let light shine out of darkness' made his light shine in our hearts to give us the light of the knowledge of the glory of God in the face of Christ" (2 Cor 4:5).* Here Paul sees himself as an authentic, Christ-proclaiming *servant* of his audience, the Corinthians.

If we're truly to be a servant of our audience, it means that we will seek to meet them "on their turf" as much as we possibly can while still operating with authenticity. We must study our audience and know their cultural language and "hot buttons" that might turn them off to our message. This means we may at times need to put our personal desires and tastes aside to more effectively communicate. Realize also that we cease to be relevant to our audience when we are being unreal or inauthentic. The greatest performance devoid of authentic love (heart) is just a noisy gong! It's easy to create a pragmatic, utilitarian program and call it art, but God calls us to more than that. He calls us to loving attitudes in all of our artistic expressions and persuasion.

As *servant-artists*, we must be willing to give up our preferences and rights for the sake of others, to effectively communicate truth and to love them. We must also realize that we are each uniquely gifted for certain audiences. You will likely be most relevant and effective with those audiences you connect with and who connect with you—those with similar experiences or interests. This doesn't mean, however, that you should only play or cater to those audiences. God may very well lead you to share with people you feel very unqualified to reach. As servants we should take every God-led opportunity we can to share His truth with others. One look at Paul's life and we see that he pursued every opportunity God gave him to share the truth, often at great personal expense and suffering (Col 1:24-28).

Attention and Active Engagement

Being culturally relevant begins with having the right attitude toward your audience, and then by knowing their expectations, attitudes, dreams and needs. You must be attentive to *who* your audience is. When people's initial expectations are met or surpassed in regard to your art, you gain their trust and their willingness to explore further. Once you've gained their trust you can begin to actively engage them in your story by sharing more of yourself.

Today just like the days of Christ, we live in a storytelling culture. It's not just a matter of presenting abstract truth to people, but of sharing how that truth intersects with our lives. Many people these days have their radar up whenever they hear talk about God. They want to know if it's real or if it's just an angle to get them to give or serve or do something. People want to hear how our "version of the truth," as they might put it, has changed our lives and our reasons for believing. And more than ever, they're looking for authenticity. Being authentic is the foundation of acceptable persuasion, and care must be taken to communicate your authenticity in a way that can be understood. This means doing your work to understand your audience.

Here are a few questions that could impact how you present your message.

1. What is my audience's primary worldview? Is it humanistic? Is it pluralistic? Does it include God, the God of the Bible or of the Koran, Buddha, etc.? Does it accept a supernatural world? What percentages believe what?

2. Is my audience generally open to change? What are the barriers they might have to hearing my story? Hearing God's story?

3. Are there circumstances, physical or emotional, that I should be aware of that would distract them from hearing or accepting what I'm saying? For example, if you are talking to teens in prison, what might their issues be?

4. What is it about my story that my audience specifically can relate to? Are there stories, events, issues locally I should be aware of that may be on their minds?

5. Am I praying and asking/listening to God about any things I should share? (Remember, it's God who changes people hearts.)

6. Am I relying on the power of the Gospel to change lives and presenting it in a compelling way? Remember that it is not our efforts or our story but God's story that changes people. [37] This goes for believers and non-believers alike.

Felt Needs

Another way to approach persuasion is to consider the audience's felt needs and their real needs. Felt need questions are: What is my audience expecting? What do they want to experience emotionally? What are their needs? Do they simply want to have fun and rock out? Will it be formal or casual? Will they be tired? Hungry? Will they be happy to be there or a captive audience (like prisoners or soldiers, etc.)? The arts and music in particular have the ability to speak to people's felt needs and break down the barriers that would prevent them from considering truth.

It is also important to clearly identify who your target audience is, especially if you have an audience of mixed generations or varied backgrounds. Are they teenagers, 30-somethings, poor, rich, etc.? Inherent in this is also the fact that you will probably speak less persuasively to those outside of your target. Sometimes those outside can become confused or even offended so, as much as possible it is important to communicate to these folks who you are really reaching out to. It is incumbent on us as communicators to be as flexible as possible to find common ground with our audience.

Real Needs

Once people's felt needs and expectations begin to be met, you begin to gain trust so that you can speak to their real needs or the truth you feel constrained by love to communicate. Here too it is important to clearly and concisely articulate your goal. What exactly do you want to communicate or persuade people to do? Remember that people do not want vague generalities about life; they need something that is real that will specifically challenge their lives, or at least their perspective. Can you put into a sentence what you want people to understand, feel or experience?

Once you know *what* you want to communicate and *where* your audience is in regard to that truth, then determine *how* you can move them from where they are or what they currently believe to where you want them to be. It is tempting to give so much information that you leave people feeling like they're drinking from a fire hose and squelch their thirst for any more. It is much better to give people just enough to challenge or change their lives but to also leave them hungry for more. Jesus did this all the time. Notice how often people came to Jesus asking questions. And notice how often Jesus answered with questions rather than just stating propositional truths. He wanted people to think for themselves and not just blindly accept whatever He said. He respected his audience, challenged them with stories and questions, and met not only their felt needs (food, rest, etc.) but also their real (spiritual, relational) needs.

3.Allowing for the God Factor

When it comes to life change, ultimately there is only One who can truly change our lives. It is not our art or music that is the transforming agent in people's lives. Nor is it your own personal charisma or lack thereof that changes people's hearts. Rather, it is God's truth and His Spirit. This is called the "God factor." His blessings may or may not be on your presentation and gifts, but His blessing is always on His truth. If you're hoping to persuade and authentically love people, God has to be involved. God can (and often does) take our meager attempts and multiplies the impact to reach far beyond what we can imagine. Sometimes He moves in amazing ways in spite of our poor planning or performance—another reminder that He changes lives for His glory, not ours. This is what makes serving Him so exciting. We can take no credit for changing people's lives. When His Spirit is working by His grace, lives are changed—despite ourselves. It's always been that way, and yet the arts can be a *means* of His grace toward people's hearts.

What are the greatest hindrances to having authentic impact?

Of course there are many, but here are three I believe derail us as artists in particular.

Me? Impact People Through Music?

Pride

This attribute is often a tough one for artists. It is so easy to take our cues from non-believers when it comes to our attitudes about our gifts and accomplishments. But we mustn't leave God out of the picture. Pride and love cannot coexist. Pride insists on exalting itself above others. It insists it's always right. It seeks its own praise and its own way. It claims its way is always right. And "pride comes before a fall."

Pride must be replaced with humility. Having humility is key to allowing God's love to invade our lives and find expression through us. Humility admits failure and need. Humility recognizes the possibility of not being "right." Humility realizes that God is greater than all and therefore should be feared, trusted and loved. Humility trusts in God's control and care, which allows you to put others ahead of yourself. "With humility of mind let each of you regard one another as more important than yourself" (Phil 2:3). Humility is the state of the heart that allows you to trust in God's love for you personally—His control, His goodness, His power—so you can give that love to others freely. A humble person sees himself as God sees him and seeks to see God and others as they are. And this is the path to be blessed. Jesus said, "Blessed are the poor in spirit (humble), for theirs is the Kingdom of God" (Matt 5:3).

Self-centeredness

The opposite of love is selfishness, not hatred. Just as you can't be proud and humble at the same time, so you can't truly be loving and selfish at the same time. The New Testament calls us to this type of revolutionary love. Jesus reminds us that we must deny ourselves to be part of His revolution, and take up our cross and follow Him. Paul reminds us to "do nothing from selfishness or empty conceit." Earlier in this passage he says, "If you have any encouragement from being united with Christ, if any comfort from his love, if any fellowship with the Spirit, if any tenderness and compassion, then make my joy complete by being like-minded, having the same love, being one in spirit and purpose" (Phil 2;1,2).

How do we come by this kind of love? Jesus shows us the way: *"As the Father has loved me, so have I loved you. Abide in my love"(Jn 15:9)*. Jesus experienced the Father's love intimately, every day (*"as the Father has loved me"*). I think this is one reason you see Him prioritizing His time with the Father in solitude. There He met with the Father and experienced His love, had His burden lifted, and got His direction for the day or next phase of ministry. Having experienced God, he moved out into the world. I would challenge you to do a study of love in the New Testament. You will find your life being revolutionized! This is why He further encouraged His disciples to "abide in my love." And what does abide mean? One commentator has this to say: *"He's not saying, 'Continue to love Me,' but, 'continue in the possession and enjoyment of My love to you'"[38]* How can we expect to be loving if we don't take time to "possess our possessions" or enjoy His love? Again, this calls for some changes in how we approach our time, energy and resources.

Lack of Preparation

This could be a fruit of the previous two hindrances, but it bears mentioning. It takes extra attention to not only prepare musically, but also to study your audience and build your program. You must also work through spoken parts in your program. The things you *say* (greeting, transitions, stories, etc.) and your *attitude* are very important to your communication. If you fail to prepare here, you most likely miss your opportunity to relate effectively to your audience.

The benefits of using our gifts to impact others

Using our gifts with others-focus and humility results in:

Me? Impact People Through Music?

Personal gratification

Knowing your art helps people find answers to their problems, whether personal, relational, spiritual or otherwise, is incredibly fulfilling. Personal fulfillment is a result of helping others through our gifts; God designed it that way! We have to be careful, however, that fulfillment itself is not our primary motivation as this would violate love. Remember, we can unknowingly slip into finding our identity from how we use our gifts or from others' affirmation. Fulfillment is simply a byproduct of following God's way, but it should not be the goal of our lives or service. Often the fulfillment or gratification of using our gifts may not come until we see Jesus and hear Him say, "Well done, good and faithful artist-servant," which leads me to the next point. My greatest joys since I've been a Christian have come from seeing people's lives touched through my life. Whether it's family members, friends from school, work, church, or somewhere else, hearing that God has used me in their lives gives me great encouragement and joy. God's grace is truly evident and amazing in these instances!

Eternal significance

I'm not talking here about personal significance. If you are in Christ, your significance is found in what He's done for you on the cross. (I highly recommend *The Search for Significance* by Robert McGee or *Waking the Dead* by John Eldredge to discover more about this.) I'm talking here about *works* that have eternal significance. Did you know that what you do with your time, energy, money and gifts can have eternal significance?

Jesus was clear about the eternal benefits of using our gifts to expand His Kingdom in the power of His Sprit. We don't hear much about this in the modern world, but it is a main theme of the New Testament. Clearly our "works" will be judged. Some will go up in smoke; others will be as silver, gold and precious stones. The NT writers knew the reality of the eternal Kingdom and that's why they exhort and plead with us to seek God's will. They remind us that "we are his workmanship, created in Christ Jesus for good works, which God prepared beforehand, that we should walk in them." [39] There is great benefit in knowing you are living your life for more than the temporal praise of men or material comfort (1 Cor 15:58).

Peace

If you are living a life of love, you will experience peace in your life with God. You may or may not have peace with others, though you should strive for it. But, if you love people in God's way, you will experience His peace. Loving God and others authentically results in peace. This was the mode of Paul's life and he encouraged the Philippians to live like him: *"The things you have learned and received and heard and seen in me, practice these things, and the God of peace will be with you."* (Phil4:9).

Are there more benefits? Most definitely! God will have many tailor-made blessings for you as you walk in His plan for your life and gifts. The Bible is filled with promises for those who surrender their lives and gifts to God and His purposes. As you look back on your life, you will not regret that you used your gifts to authentically impact others with His love.

"No eye has seen, no ear has heard, no mind has conceived what God has prepared for those who love Him." (1 Corinthians 2:9)

To recap, here are this chapter's main points:

- As artists we should authentically use our gifts to move people spiritually! Our message should:
  - Please God - we should have a clear conscience
  - Influence others toward good, not evil
  - Be honest

Me? Impact People Through Music?

- Reflect God's heart
- Marks of Authentic Persuasion are:
  - Cultural Relevance
  - Sharing the truth in love
  - Allowing for the God factor
- We must recognize and eliminate hinderances to having an authentic impact such as pride, self-centeredness and lack of preparation.
- We should take joy in the benefits of impacting others spiritually.

What a privilege it is use our gifts to influence and even persuade people toward a real life!

Endnote:

Key Questions for an Audience-Moving Program:

Events fall into three categories:

- Non- Persuasive - This program is simply to provide music with no programming or persuasive intent. This might be dinner music or social background music, etc. Okay, even elevator music.

- Entertainment - The goal here is to give people a positive experience. This may include a wide range of musical moods in the concert, but the end result is to move people emotionally—to make them feel like they've been highly entertained or taken on a journey with no challenge to change.

- Persuasive - There are many ways that artists seek to persuade people. This includes intellectual, social, political, spiritual and relational areas of life. These programs include elements that are chosen intentionally to get people's attention and make them think and be persuaded to adopt the artists' message. These programs (if musical) usually include entertaining and emotionally moving elements.

There is a continuum here as you may see. Different programs and program elements will have differing degrees of intentional persuasion. Here are questions to ask in developing your program.

1. What is the purpose of your concert/event?
    *   State your goal. It can range from simply providing background music to entertainment to communicating eternal truths.... It's also good to note that within a concert or event there are also sub-purposes, which should hopefully compliment your overall purpose... like entertaining moments that lead to poignant reflection, etc.
    *   Are you and your host agreed upon your purpose? It's always good to be clear here, especially if you want to be invited back! Chances are that you have been hired or selected because of what or how they think you will communicate.

2. Who's your audience? - This is a very important question, especially if your plan is to significantly impact people. Some things to consider are:
    *   Age, stylistic preferences, peer pressure People more than ever identify themselves with certain styles of music. Is yours acceptable? If not, should you make a disclaimer? Cancel your appearance? (Hopefully not!)
    *   Energy levels and attentiveness. Will they be alert? Tired? Hungry? This may affect the length of your program.
    *   Environmental dynamics and distractions, e.g., room, crowd, noise, sound system.

Me? Impact People Through Music?

- Worldview, i.e. assumptions people might make about you as a performer, the content of your message, barriers they may have to listening to your message and your music.
- Expectations. What is your audience expecting? Answering this question will help you know where to begin your programming, to build on their anticipation or dispel their assumptions.

3. How will I authentically communicate?

- Are my intentions good? Authenticity here is important for lots of reasons, and it affects your *influence* more than anything else. Especially in our post-modern culture, people can smell inauthenticity and will put up a barrier to any inauthentic persuasive attempts.
- Is my process good? i.e., the activities leading too your end product. Let your core values drive your process. Once you've identified your core values, they should act as signposts at every decision. People will sense your "realness" and believability and hopefully respect the integrity of your product.
- How will I love and show love to my audience on and off stage? Am I praying for them? Am I maintaining appropriate relationships?
- Am I trusting God to work through me? Don't forget the God factor! Missionary William Carey coined the phrase, "Expect great things from God, attempt great things for God."

Follow-up Questions

Chapter 6: Me? Impact People Through Music?

1. Do you agree it is good to try to influence or persuade others by your art? Why or why not?

2. What guides the messages you put in your music? Do you agree our conscience and God's truth should set the boundaries for our expression? Why or why not?

3. The point is made that love (God's love) should characterize our attitudes and actions toward others, even through our art. What hindrances do you find in creating love-motivated art? (Pride and self-centeredness, etc.)

4. Pray and ask God to show you how you could use your gifts to impact others. It may be by starting a project or joining a band.

5. Cultural relevance, loving your audience and presenting God's truth (the gospel) are key elements of moving an audience spiritually. Which of these are strongest in your events? Which are weakest?

6. What one step could you take to improve your impact and communication skills? E.g., Take a class, get a coach, evaluate your performances.

7. Off-stage Authenticity

"What we do off stage eventually affects what happens on stage."

If you're authentic at all, you're authentic off stage. Examples certainly in modern culture and throughout history show that it is what is done off stage that really proves what we're made of. And what we do off stage eventually affects what happens on stage.

If authentic artists are people who knows their *giftedness*, develops their *skill*, and create their art from a growing, "spiritually alive" *heart*, then to have a growing heart means this authenticity eventually will affect every area of their life. Authentic artists are people who have found their true purpose in life, not just as a artist but in all areas of life.

If you're a musician, think of the non-music-related areas of your life and ask yourself what it means to be authentic in *these* areas. Examples might be relationships, school, work, other hobbies, or sports. Are there gifts you can develop to help you grow? Are there ways you can let your heart be changed in these areas?

The Challenge to Grow

Jesus' goal for us is to be who we already are in Him and for our behavior to reflect God's love and will for our lives. Even Jesus Christ had to grow in wisdom and stature and favor with God and man (Luke 2:52, Heb 5:8). If He needed to grow and learn, shouldn't we also? God takes this seriously and often lets things happen in our lives to remind us that we still need to be growing and pliable in His hands. The apostle Paul worked to grow in God's calling for his life: *"But by the grace of God I am what I am, and his grace toward me was not in vain. On the contrary, I worked harder than any of them, though it was not I, but the grace of God that is with me" (1 Cor 15:10)*

Some off-stage growth areas to consider:
These areas can be grouped into 3 primary areas: personal growth, vocation and relationships.
Personal Growth:

- Spiritual– growing in your love and knowledge of God and usefulness to Him
- Personal development– emotional, mental, musical
- Physical– diet, exercise, health

Vocation (Calling):

- Work and service in the world
- Financial– giving, saving, spending decisions

Relationships:

- Family–parents, siblings, spouses, significant others, children
- Social influence–friendships, neighbors, team/band members, community impact

The point here is not that we need to be perfect in all of these areas. In fact don't even try! The test of authenticity however, is in how we respond to failure—to humbly admit when you've blown it and to seek to grow more and more into what God has called/created you to be. In short, it's letting our walk match our new life in Christ!

Off-stage Authenticity

The Acid Test

The acid test for authenticity is ultimately in relationships. Even our vocational calling is first to our 'Caller" - God, and second to our work. God created us as relational beings and to Him relationships are the most significant part of life. Our relationships with others, with God and even ourselves form the fabric of our lives. Being "in right relationship" is the heart of what Jesus has called us to:

> *You shall love the Lord your God with all your heart and with all your soul and with all your mind. This is the great and first commandment. And the second is like it: You shall love your neighbor as yourself. (Matt 22:37)*

Personal Growth and Vocation

Personal growth includes the physical, personal development (emotional, mental), and spiritual areas of your life. It is out of your relationship with God (spiritual), physical ability and personal development that you relate to others in your life. Growing in the spiritual area has been touched on in chapter 3. There are also many books and online resources to help you grow in physical and personal development. Vocation is also a very important area. This book won't address this but again, there are many resources to help. Please see the appendix.

To have authentic relationships with others is often a greater challenge than personal development or vocational issues. Sometimes we create the problems in our relationships and sometime others create them. How we pursue, develop and manage our relationships is probably the greatest indication of our maturity.

Authentic Relationships

True authenticity is reflected in having authentic relationships. C.S. Lewis wrote:

Love anything and your heart will be wrung and possibly broken. If you want to make sure of keeping it intact you must give it to no one, not even an animal. Wrap it carefully round with hobbies and little luxuries; avoid all entanglements. Lock it up safe in the casket or coffin of your selfishness. But in that casket – safe, dark, motionless, airless – it will change. It will not be broken; it will become unbreakable, impenetrable, and irredeemable. To love is to be vulnerable.

Lewis understood perhaps more than most, that isolation is a downward spiral that leads to lifelessness. And yet, later in his life he experienced new-birth spiritually and he also allowed God to change his relationships. To become involved in significant relationships means we will face disappointments and conflicts as well as incredible life-giving, even inspiring joys and friendships.

So what truths has God revealed about relationships? What did He have in mind when He created us? Let's take a look at what God's original design was for our relational world. Once we see what authentic relationships should look like, it will be much easier to see where there is inauthenticity in our relationships. We naturally look to our parents or family for relational models, but God invites us to look to His heart and His plan as our model.

People with authentic relationships live by these truths. They:
1. Value people
2. Love God above all others
3. Love others unconditionally
4. Choose friends wisely
5. Pursue resolution when there's conflict

6. Speak truth and give grace to one another

7. Know their own strengths and share them with others; know their own weaknesses and receive others' strengths into their lives

8. Pursue God's will and maintain appropriate boundaries and levels of vulnerability

Let's go deeper into these points:.

1. Value people

People are eternal

Notice in the creation account, God created man and woman in His image. Unlike any other part of creation, we are unique. We reflect the Creator in that we are eternal, we are to be holy, and we embody all of the attributes of God as Jesus did. God created man and said it was very good. Therefore, we mustn't treat people as things or commodities but as His high point of creation. Here too, we only begin to see dimly the magnificence of God's creation in us— even though we're fallen creatures, there is still the imprint of our Father Creator on each person. C.S. Lewis said that if we should see a person's true glory—the glory they were given before the fall—we might even be tempted to bow and worship them! The Bible is clear—we are eternal and we all will spend eternity somewhere. Do you realize you're going to spend eternity with your fellow believers? Even those with whom you have a conflict? Sometimes, this perspective helps me pursue loving someone and pursuing peace in our relationship, knowing that in heaven I will be living with them *forever*!

People matter

This is the overwhelming message of the Gospel. No greater price could have been paid for our salvation. Jesus gave his life for us, that He may bring us to God—to enjoy Him forever—people of every race, color and background. They matter to Him. Do they matter to me? Do I care?

God created each person with unique gifts and talents, personalities and backgrounds. While we mustn't accept people's behavior when it's sinful, we must not devalue or denigrate someone or place ourselves above another person. Do you see people as a valuable creation of God, for whom Christ died? We must see past someone's bad behavior to the potential and the person God wishes to call forth in their hearts.

2. Love God above all others

This is perhaps where our original parents got it wrong, and we still do today. We were created first and foremost for God—to know Him and love Him. We can experience supernatural joy when He is our first love, above anything or anyone else. When we place another before Him, we get in trouble. Pride caused Eve and Adam to place God lower than He is. They lowered their view of Him and believed the lie of Satan. They wanted control, perhaps they wanted to impress each other, or wanted to escape their responsibilities, or to take a short cut to a good thing (one definition of sin). At any rate they chose to transgress and forfeited intimacy with God.

When things are good in a relationship, the tendency is often to begin to put that person above all else (Idolatry), to look to that relationship for things that only our intimacy with God can bring. And then there are many times in every relationship when loving and valuing the other person is very difficult. But to have a good relationship we mustn't base it on how "loveable" the other person is at the moment. In essence, it's only as we find our deepest needs being met in our relationship with God that we are free to love others in a healthy way. Often you may find your relationship with God to be the only real reason for loving someone, especially in difficult situations. Your love for another person, i.e.. your obedience to God, mustn't be based on another's response (their love or enthusiasm, etc.). It must be based on your desire to please God above all else.

After our first year of marriage, my wife and I agreed we couldn't imagine living together without Christ at the center of our relationship. It seemed inconceivable to us that others could be happy without His presence in their lives as their first love. Knowing Him both enriches our "high times" and gives us grace for each other in our "low times."

Jesus made this "first love" principle clear to his disciples in Luke 14:26, stating that our love for others should look like hatred compared to our love for Him. In other words, our love for Him should far surpass our love for others.

3. Love others unconditionally

"I tell you, the more I think, the more I feel that there is nothing more truly artistic than to love people" (Vincent Van Gogh.)[40]

This point follows from the previous point because to love unconditionally is to love with God's love. The Bible identifies four primary types of love, the most important being God's unconditional love called "agape." This is the type of love that drove Jesus to the cross for us and raised Him from the dead. It is this supernatural love that is to characterize Christ followers as well. This type of love continues on regardless of how much the person deserves or has earned it. It says, "I will love you regardless of your response or our history. I will think, say and do what is most loving toward you, not looking to merely meet my needs or wants." It means being tender and tough when appropriate. A friend of mine rightly said, "Unconditional love is the lubricant that makes the machine of relationships work."

Jesus and the apostles called the earlier church to stand out in their pagan world by depth of their relationships, i.e., their love for one another (e.g. Jn 14:35, Phil 2:1-5). It is also this unconditional love that is to compel us to reach out to the hurting world. In 2 Corinthians 5:14-21, we see that this is God's and our mission in the world: to bring people out of their hopelessness and "lostness" into peace with Him and a new life in Him! This is at the heart of God's work in the world—loving people, believers and pre-believers—toward wholeness in Christ. The apostle Paul wrote:

> *Christ's love controls us. Since we believe that Christ died for all, we also believe that we have all died to our old life. He died for everyone so that those who receive his new life will no longer live for themselves. Instead, they will live for Christ, who died and was raised for them. So we have stopped evaluating others from a human point of view. At one time we thought of Christ merely from a human point of view. How differently we know him now! This means that anyone who belongs to Christ has become a new person. The old life is gone; a new life has begun! And all of this is a gift from God, who brought us back to himself through Christ. And God has given us this task of reconciling people to him. (2 Cor 5:14-18 NLT)*

Part of the key to loving people unconditionally is to see them as God sees them—not looking at outward appearances as this passage says. But rather, to seek God's perspective and join Him in His mission of love. Loving people well takes a lifetime to learn, and it certainly takes God's Spirit to do it well. As Van Gogh said, it is truly an art, and it requires supernatural power.

4. Choose friends wisely

"In everyone's life, at some time, our inner fire goes out. It is then burst into flame by an encounter with another human being. We should all be thankful for those people who rekindle the inner spirit" (Albert Schweitzer). [41]

Off-stage Authenticity

It may seem a bit antithetical to say we should love all people regardless of differences, and then to discriminate when it comes to who we choose to relate with the closest—our friends. The fact, is however, that we do not have the capacity to love on such a grand scale as God does. We are not able to relate to everyone at the same level, and if we try we end up not only disappointing others, but also becoming shallow and missing out on the growth that comes from deeper relationships. This is part of the reason God has given us boundaries in our relationships. He knows what is best for us.

We naturally have more affinity with certain people than others. Some people give us energy and encouragement, and others may be more neutral or even draining to us. There are many examples of friendships in the Bible, e.g., David and Jonathan, Ruth and Naomi, Paul and Timothy. Jesus had not only his disciples but also the three, Peter, James and John, with whom He took into his deepest confidence.

The book of proverbs also has much to say about friendships:
"A friend loves at all times and a brother is born for adversity" (Pro 17:17)
"Faithful are the wounds of a friend…" (Pro 27:6)
"The sweetness of a friend comes from his earnest counsel" (Pro 27:9)
"Iron sharpens iron, so one man sharpens another" (Pro 27:17)
"Without counsel plans fail, with many advisers they succeed" (Pro 15:22)

The difference between an acquaintance, a friend, a lover and all of the various levels of relationship is trust and commitment. The level of trust and commitment in your relationships determines the level of your involvement. It is often good to reflect on the commitments you've made in your relationships and ask if you are living up to them, and whether you have mutual expectations. Ask also if your trust and intimacy are growing as they should.

Here are just a few questions to ponder:

1. What is my friendship capacity? Am I spread too thin or too much of a hermit?
2. Are my friendships good for me? Are my friends benefiting?
3. Are there appropriate boundaries with the opposite sex?
4. Do I need to be more discerning about others' impact on me?
5. Am I investing in my relationships as I should?
6. Who can I learn from? Who can I mentor?

"If we are privileged to explore our new horizons with other painters through brush, paper and pigment, we are truly blessed" (Michele Cooper).[42]

5. Pursue resolution when there's conflict

With greater commitment comes greater vulnerability and expectation, as well as the potential for conflict. Actually, conflict is a given; you can expect to find it in nearly any long-term relationship. Conflict happens when there is an unmet expectation of what a relationship should be. Sometimes it's just a miscommunication or a misunderstanding, but at times it can be a significant transgression, causing pain and leaving a deep scar.

It is when there is a sense of a real divide in your relationship with someone that you must seek resolution. If you sense someone has something against you, go to them, try to clear the fog and come to peace with the person. If you are offended by someone else's behavior to the point that it affects your thoughts and feelings toward them, go to them, seek peace and reconciliation. It is evident from the Bible that we are to pursue reconciliation regardless of who caused the offense (Mat 5:23,24; 18:15).

Some quick principles about conflict resolution:

- Spend time getting God's perspective on the person and the problem. Seek to understand what the real issue is, pray before talking, believe the best of the person (1 Cor 13) and cleanse your heart of impure motives and thoughts (1 Jn 1:9). Get your anger under control and let love, not anger rule your actions. How you feel is the result of an issue you need to address. If you just let your emotions fly, you'll only cloud the issue (Eph 4:26,27).

- Determine to make positive emotional investments in your relationships so that when you have to make a withdrawal (say something difficult), there is an understanding of your love for them.

- Don't attack the person, attack the problem. Don't use accusatory language like "You are _____." Rather, say "When you do _____, it makes me feel _____."

- Don't assume you understand what the other person is saying. Repeat it back to them for clarification, like "What I hear you saying is _____."

- Be willing to agree to disagree over an issue. Sometimes we just have different opinions and we need to respect each other regardless. Peace is the goal in any conflict, not necessarily agreement.

- If possible, include God in your conversation and pray together, He desires to be at the center of your most significant relationships and He is ultimately your source of love, peace and healing.

- Forgive. To forgive is to release the offender of "payback" and to be released of your feelings of revenge and resentment. Forgiveness frees the forgiver and can help the offender move forward. This does not mean that your trust in the relationship is necessarily restored. Trust is earned over time. Forgiveness is granted as an act of the will.

As Christ-followers, we have no choice but to seek peace in our relationships. We may not always have peace, because the other party may simply not want to reconcile. But it is our responsibility to pursue resolution with others (Rom 12:18). After all, that is what God did with us (Col 3:13)!

6. Speak truth and give grace to one another

God gives us grace and He also speaks truth into our lives, confronting wrong ambitions, attitudes and actions. This is part of how we grow up in Christ-likeness. And God's method to communicate His truth to us is—you guessed it—through our relationships! He wants to speak to you through His word by His Spirit. He will also use others to speak truth into your life, and He wants to use *you* to speak truth into your friends' lives.

The willingness to speak honestly about what we see in each others' lives is critical to our growth. It takes courageous love and commitment to do so, and I'm sure you can see how this may also cause conflict! After all, we want to be comfortable and safe with our friends, which we should be. However, it takes more than that to grow personally and in our relationships.

More questions for you to ponder:

1. Do I believe the best of others and have the attitude of Christ toward others? (Phil 2:5)
2. Do I receive "truth telling" from other people with a humble, teachable heart?
3. Do I share truth in love with others appropriately, as God leads me, without an "agenda" of trying to change someone? God is the one who changes people!
4. Do my friends and I have the same values when it comes to relationships? Perhaps a discussion about this would be

appropriate. Are we/Am I willing to pursue growth personally even if it means hearing some hard things?

7. Know their own strengths and share them with others; know their own weaknesses and receive others' strengths into their lives.

This may seem obvious, but you must exercise your gifts and recognize you need other people and their gifts in order to be successful. This is part of God's plan for building His Kingdom into your life, your family, friendships, and community. You can discover your gifts and strengths from personality tests, spiritual gift assessments, feedback from others, and your experiences. Seek to understand how you're wired. You are unique!

The key to receiving other's gifts and strengths is having humility. Paul warns us, "*Don't think you are better than you really are. Be honest in your evaluation of yourselves, measuring yourselves by the faith God has given us. Just as our bodies have many parts and each part has a special function, so it is with Christ's body. We are many parts of one body, and we all belong to each other. In his grace, God has given us different gifts for doing certain things well*" (Rom 12:3-5). See also 1 Cor12:12-25, 1 Peter 4:10,11

8. Pursue God's will and maintain appropriate boundaries in their relationships.

Relationships are a gift from God. No one probably knew that better than Adam, the first man. God showed Adam his need for a mate by having him name all of the animals. He saw that unlike the animals there was no mate for him in all of creation. Even in his unfallen state, he needed a relationship with another human being. And God brought it to Him in His way and His time.

The same is true for us; we need relationships. And God desires to be glorified in the "process" as well as the "product" of finding and developing our relationships. Speaking of product, perhaps vision is a better word. You may have a vision for of the kind of relationships you want to be in, i.e. band of brothers, good friends, or even marriage, but remember that God wants you to be faithful and to learn where you are. It's easy to dream of someday having an incredible marriage, for instance, but still be complacent and not do anything toward becoming a great spouse today.

Here are some commitment/vulnerability questions to ponder for your relationships/friendships:

1. What are my desires (godly) for my relationships?
2. Have I prayed about them, continued to seek discernment?
3. Who do I sense He may be leading me to?
4. What actions should I take to pursue a relationship?
5. Have I determined healthy boundaries in this relationship? (especially if with the opposite sex)
6. How will I keep the Lord at the center of our relationship?

Rubbing shoulders rubs off!

It's great to know all eight of these points, but the real test is how you apply them to your life. Probably the best way to grow in this area is to be around people who really understand and can model to you what authentic relationships should look like. The place we should see this most is in the Church, is it not? Churches and especially small groups can be a great place to observe and develop authentic relationships.

Jesus felt deeply about authentic relationships for His disciples: "By this all people will know that you are my disciples, if you have love for one another" (Jn 14:35), and in His prayer at the end of his life: "I ask...

that they may all be one, just as you, Father, are in me, and I in you, that they also may be in us, so that the world may believe that you have sent me" (Jn 17:21). If you've never done this before, look at a list of all the "one another" passages in the New Testament; it's overwhelming, and a huge challenge to authentic living.

Why is this so hard? Why do I see others struggling so much?

If you've grown up around authentic relationships, your have been blessed indeed. If your parents and siblings were committed to good relationships, you entered life already with a lot to offer others. Chances are, however, that you entered adulthood with a deficit of modeling and perhaps baggage that makes having true, authentic relationships a real challenge. And, the fact is that even for those with great family and church backgrounds, having authentic relationships is be a challenge. Why? Because we are all imperfect people, who relate imperfectly. And because the enemy (satan) attacks our relationships regularly.

Both of these points demand that we be vigilant to fight for healthy relationships. They don't just happen. And if it seems like it's effortless and you'll never have any challenges living with someone, just wait! Relationships left untended tend to drift. They are like gardens that must be worked to keep the weeds out and watered to keep the soil fresh. All people want to have great relationships, do they not? However, not all are willing to do the work necessary to have great relationships. Our calling as believers is to do the work!

"Beloved let us love one another, for love is from God, and whoever loves had been born of God and knows God." (1 Jn 4:7,8)

Authentic Relationships in Marriage

If you're married, part of the reason God has you together is that you might model to the world authenticity as a couple. This is expressly stated in the Old and New Testament and we must take it seriously. Don't forget the purpose of your marriage! Satan delights in getting us to settle for less than God's desires for our lives and relationships.

An authentic marriage is a hugely powerful tool for God in the world. Paul's words in Ephesians 5:22-33 remind us that our relationships with each other (husband and wife) are to model Christ's relationship with His Church. How much grace and love does He give to His church? How much did He suffer and submit to in order to build His church? That's part of our calling as husbands. How much is the church to submit to Christ's love and leadership? What is the church's attitude to be toward serving the Lord? That's part of the wife's calling to her husband. This type of mutual submission and love in a marriage is revolutionary in today's world. An authentic marriage models to all who see it a hugely attractive picture of God's kingdom.

We all know it takes work to develop an authentic marriage. Let me challenge you to be highly vigilant about it! In fact, be proactive about it: go to seminars*, read books, pray together regularly, and communicate every day from your hearts. Place your marriage's health and unity above your work and art, because God does. If you have great success in work or your music but have a dying marriage, it will undermine any impact you are seeking to have with others and it will also grieve God.

- Do you know what the purpose of your marriage is in God's eyes?
- Do you know what God's agenda is for your marriage these days?
- Do you have agreed-upon goals to keep growing together?
- Are you committed to a cause greater than yourselves and your marriage?

Early in our engagement, my wife and I understood that the purpose of our marriage was to:

- Reign spiritually with Christ – claiming the authority in Christ over satan's lies and agenda

- Reflect His life to each other and the world around us
- Reproduce a godly heritage – not just physically but also by having a spiritual impact in others' lives

These points have served as a compass for our marriage. Seeking to follow God's agenda has been a huge blessing. It has brought us into a life and marriage much bigger than had we just lived for the status quo. Now, having adult children, we find God's plan continuing to infuse life and purpose into our marriage as we keep pursuing having an impact in others lives for Christ together. (I highly recommend the Family LIfe Ministry's "Weekend to Remember" conferences - www.familylife.com. Go more than once!)

Application

There you have it … easy to write about, hard to live. Having authentic relationships is a lifetime project, but nothing will give you greater fulfillment in the end. We are hard-wired for this and everyone, if not openly, secretly longs for authentic relationships. As you know, the arts are always illustrating this! For example, the Lord of the Rings is a great adventure movie, but isn't the story really built around the relational stories of Frodo and Sam and others? *Saving Private Ryan* is a great war story, but isn't it really built around the teamwork it took to save Private Ryan? *Slumdog Milliionaire* is a great story too, and it's built around the evolution of three friendships. Other movies are even more obvious, and we could go on. But I think you get the idea. Let's write our own stories of authentic relationships, which will shine bright in a dark world.

People with authentic relationships:
- Value people
- Love God above all others

- Love others unconditionally
- Choose friends wisely
- Pursue resolution when there's a conflict
- Are truth telling and grace giving
- Know their own strengths and share them with others; know their own weaknesses and receive others' strengths into their lives.
- Pursue God's will and maintain appropriate boundaries and levels of vulnerability in their relationships

More off-stage points

Develop a Plan

As an exercise to expand your thinking outside of your art, write a statement in each of the off-stage areas to define what growth might look like. Try to think in terms of who God has made you to be in Christ, and what He has called you to do as a result. Our actions are always a result of what we really believe to be true about ourselves and God. Also your personal growth process will evolve as you discover more and more of your strengths and what God has called you to do. Just as Paul said he "buffeted" his body to accomplish his calling, so you too will need to pursue a plan to grow. Develop a plan you can make your own and live with. How you approach your "growth paradigm" may be completely different from my example that follows, but just remember that the point of it all is to actually *grow*! Growth doesn't just happen. God has given us a mind, desires and His Spirit to guide and empower us. One person wisely said, "Goals are dreams with a deadline."

Here's my example of a one-year plan for eight areas of life, beginning with my mission statement. Note that your plan will be different on many points.

Off-stage Authenticity

My Mission: To glorify God by accomplishing the work He's given me to do in the Holy Spirit's power while becoming the person He's created me to be in Christ.

My Goals:

Spiritual: living life out of life-giving fellowship with Jesus.

   Be: Man of God

   Do: This year's goals (measurable, dated)

Physical: Being fit, healthy and strong.

   Be: Temple of God, steward

   Do: This year's goals (measurable, dated)

Emotional: Expressing and renewing my emotions and heart in healthy, God-honoring ways.

   Be: Child of God (son of God)

   Do: This year's goals (measurable, dated)

Personal Development: Developing and using my gifts, talents and abilities to their potential for God's glory.

   Be: Steward

   Do: This year's goals (measurable, dated) – this could include musical development!

Marriage/Family: Reigning with Jesus, reflecting Jesus, reproducing a godly heritage in oneness with my spouse.

   Be: Son, husband, father (wife, mother, etc.)

   Do:

      With my spouse—This year's goals (measurable, dated)

      With my children—This year's goals (measurable, dated)

      With my extended family—This year's goals (measurable, dated)

Social/Influence: Living an influential life before non-believers and society.

   Be: Salt and light – influencer, leader

   Do: This year's goals (measurable, dated)

Financial: Honoring God by how I earn, give, invest and spend my (His) money.

Be: Steward

Do: This year's goals (measurable, dated)

Vocation work/ministry: – Note: I've written a separate calling and mission statement for my life *Work/ministry:*

Calling: to be an authentic musician, servant/leader and equipper of other musicians and artists

Mission: 1) to authentically use music and the performing arts to move people spiritually toward Jesus Christ;   2) to equip artists to have authentic lives and fruitful ministries; and 3) to serve others who invest in God's Kingdom by partnering with us in ministry.

Be: Bondservant

Do: This year's goals (measurable, dated) – this may be broken down into many areas...

These dreams, desires, and goals should form the context of your year, but should also take you beyond one year. It's important to reevaluate your direction periodically and let God grow your vision and desires, as only He can do for those who seek Him.

There is a difference between desires and goals, too. You should have both. Desires are something you want and dream of. Goals are measurable and quantifiable. Goals allow accountability. They help to move you toward your desires. For example, I may desire to record a CD. But a goal says I will write three songs by October 1 for the CD. Also, don't get so caught up in your planning that you never "run your play." Likewise, don't fall for the trap that growth will "just happen" as you go your way. The verse below exhorts us to work it out—to take what we've been given (our salvation) and live it before the world. Carpe Diem!

Off-stage Authenticity

"Work out your salvation with fear and trembling for it is God who is at work in you both to will and to work for His good pleasure." (Phil 2:12,13)

Finally, I'm reminded of the apostle Paul's words to his protege, Timothy to "fan into flame the gift of God, which is in you....for God has not given a spirit of timidity but of power and love and self-control" (2Tim1:5-7) We have the power to lived changed lives!

Voices from other artists on relationships:

"There is no such thing as a 'self-made' man. We are made up of thousands of others" (George Matthew Adams). [43]

"There are high spots in all of our lives and most of them have come about through encouragement from someone else" (George Matthew Adams).[44]

"Don't walk in front of me, I may not follow. Don't walk behind me, I may not lead. Walk beside me and be my friend" (Albert Camus).[45]

"There is no wilderness like life without friends; friendship multiplies blessings and minimizes misfortunes; it is a unique remedy against adversity and it soothes the soul" (Baltasar Gracian). [46]

"Artists are often poignantly careless about making and keeping friends" (Eric Maisel). [47]

"Poets and painters need as many friends as they can get. They're good for each other. May their friendship endure and flourish" (David Masello).[48]

"Under the magnetism of friendship the modest man becomes bold; the shy, confident; the lazy, active; and the impetuous, prudent and peaceful" (William Makepeace Thackeray). [49]

Follow-up Questions

Chapter 7: Off-stage Authenticity

1. Do you have a clearly defined mission statement for your life, not just your music or art?

2. "Relationships are the acid test for our authenticity." Is there depth in your relationships and personal integrity beyond just what people see? Do you value having authentic relationships?

3. Which of the questions throughout this chapter do you need to act on?

4. How has your history impacted your ability to have authentic relationships?

5. Relationships take work and sacrifice. Who are the people God is calling you to relate with most deeply?

6. What are the greatest threats in your life to having healthy relationships?

7. What short-term goals for this year would you like or feel led to pursue? Have you put a deadline to your goals?

9. Sanity

"When it comes to sanity or insanity, authentic living or hypocritical living, enthusiastic living or burnout, the challenge is to keep our hearts fully alive."

Is it me or is life today much like trying to drink from a fire hose pushing out water at four gallons per second? It seems that while there are enormous resources and possibilities for a "maximum life" or "the life you've always wanted," modern living tries to push our minds and hearts to process more than we can handle and still live authentically. Trying to keep up on everything culturally, musically, technologically or any other way can keep us constantly living on the surface, ignoring the warning signals that our hearts may be sending us.

Think about it. Being a musician today, you can search around the world via the Internet for instruments, gigs, friends, teachers and information, as well as post your work, be accessible 24/7 to other people for sessions, lessons or information. Email, MySpace, Facebook, Twitter and a host of other Internet, cell phone and media forms vie for our time. There are more music genres today than ever before of which you may or may not feel the need to be informed. Because of the increase in consumer-oriented technology, you may need to learn new software, hardware or techniques to not only write your music but also to produce and market it online.

On top of this are all of the non-musical opportunities and demands of living in our world. There are relational needs, obligations and desires others have for you, plus financial needs, emotional, physical, spiritual and social needs you have personally, or a crisis in one area or another... the list could go on. It can leave you feeling overwhelmed just thinking about it all. And then I come along and say we should live authentically! Doesn't it sound like just another thing to add to your list of things to do?

How do you begin to sort it all out? What's really important at the end of the day?

It's all about your heart

What matters the most in living to the full is living with a fully alive heart. Living authentically is not principally about "doing"; it's about "being." It's about being in right relationship with God first. It's about being who you were created to be and relating to others in the way God has designed. Doing flows out of who we are being. And who we are "being" is all about our heart. Jesus put it this way: *"But what comes out of the mouth proceeds from the heart, and this defiles a person. For out of the heart come evil thoughts, murder, adultery, sexual immorality, theft, false witness, slander. These are what defile a person"* (Matt 15:18,19).

God looks at our heart while man looks at outward appearances. The Scriptures tell us to diligently watch over our heart, for from it flows the "springs of life"! Your heart is worth watching over. In fact, Christ died for your heart. He has redeemed you and has given you a new heart to live from... and it's worth fighting for. (Jesus is describing the "old heart" in the verse above.)

Sanity

When it comes to sanity or insanity, authentic living or hypocritical living, enthusiastic living or burnout, the challenge is to keep our hearts *fully alive*. So, how do we do that? Did Jesus have anything to say about that?

Warning: The first thing to realize is that our hearts don't necessarily respond to our 21st century way of fixing things. Our culture today wants a quick, painless, easy answer to everything. If something promises a fast, comfortable, affordable fix—whether to our waistline or our bank account—we jump on it. But when it comes to our heart, as with many other things in life, health and healing don't always come this easily or quickly.

But God has revealed to us through His word principles that we can live by to ensure we are growing toward a healthy heart and keeping away from hypocrisy. Many of these principles are not quick fixes, like taking a pill and now you're all better. Rather, it is more like a vitamin you take and practice over time, gradually bringing greater health and strength. Following are some ideas to help you guard yourself from insanity. Many books have been written on each point, but this list of suggestions will get you started.

Sanity Basics

1. Connect with God from your heart

As we discussed in chapter 3, God is most interested in a heart relationship with us. This is what Jesus was seeking when He came (Heb 12:3). It is through our hearts that God has chosen to relate to us. If we have junk in our hearts that we keep hanging on to—lies about God or ourselves, harmful habits or attitudes, i.e., sin—they create a barrier to our connection with God. If you bring your heart before God and listen to what He says, He will point out some of those things and ask you to repent. He is patient with us too, and doesn't expect perfection, but growth little by little.

David, in the Old Testament, knew God and felt safe enough in His love to say: *"Search me, O God, and know my heart. Try me and know my anxious thoughts. And see if there be any hurtful way in me, and lead me in the everlasting way"* (Ps 139:23,24).

Disciplines of the Heart

Obviously, to do what I've just described takes time. It takes time to cut through all the surface things going on in your head. It takes time to get the "RPMs" in your mind to calm down enough to listen to your deepest thoughts and emotions (your heart) and God's Spirit. It also takes wisdom to know what "disciplines" you need to help get you there.

Disciplines are described as a "means of grace" for believers. They aren't employed to gain favor from God or a better standing, but they are a means to deepen your fellowship with the Almighty, your Creator, your Lover and Friend. And while there may be times when you find you are able to encounter God with little discipline on your part, there are also times when for a variety of reasons (your own waywardness, spiritual battle, etc.), God may call you to employ more drastic disciplines like fasting or solitude to block out the things that are trying to dampen God's presence and power in your life.

Being disciplined often means saying no to certain activities—even good activities—in order to say yes to God and other better things. I hesitate to give you a list of things you should do. The danger is that we are tempted to simply check these things off our "to do" list and think we're done, without ever really listening to our heart in the process. Plus, the longer we do these things by routine, the easier it becomes to not engage or really listen to God's Spirit.

Sanity

On a practical level, however, connecting our hearts with God means prioritizing time in:

- God's Word – reading not just for information but also for inspiration or illumination, letting God speak to your heart and show you who He is, who you are in Christ. You will also gain perspective on others in your life and your circumstances.

- Worship and prayer – lifting your heart in adoration of who God is, thanking and requesting of Him your deepest desires and needs. The Lord's Prayer is a good model for this.

- Waiting in silence on Him and listening – giving God space to speak to your heart. Most people find journaling very helpful here. What is God saying to you through His Word? Through your recent experiences? Through other people (pastors, teachers, friends)? By impressions of His Spirit?

- Obeying what He shows you to do – obedience leads to knowing and loving Him more (Jn 14:21).

- Taking extended times seasonally, yearly, etc. to nourish your heart with Christ in solitude, prayer and fasting, etc.

Your relationship. That's what it gets down to. As I've seen in my own life and watched in so many other friends' lives, our failure to prioritize our relationship with God is always the reason for our failure to live authentically and experience the abundant life Jesus promised (Jn 10:10). To fail to walk in the light every day is to deplete your heart of the resources you will need for the battles you will invariably encounter.

2. Connect with other believers

"While it may feel natural to devote yourself to your creative work and succumb to feelings of separation and alienation, it nevertheless isn't a terrific idea in terms of your overall happiness and health." --Eric Maisel
50

You may not feel like living in community, but every believer has been created (and commanded) to live in significant relationships with other believers. This goes to the heart of what Jesus prayed for His disciples (Jn 17), and what God has in mind for his church. You have been created for community—for your own health. All of us have varying degrees of "relationship capacity," but all of us need at least a "band of brothers" (and sisters) from whom we can receive encouragement and to whom we can give it. Some people have great relational capacity; others become overwhelmed by more than a few significant friends. The fact still remains that you will find a much greater balance and life in your heart as you experience true fellowship with other Christ followers (1 Jn1:7). The New Testament prescribes engagement with both a body of believers, where we serve and use our gifts to build up others, as well as a more intimate, small group or one-on-one connection with mentors and protégés.

This may take a while to find, but you must not give up on it. Like fighting for your heart, fighting for true community is worth it—not only for yourself, but also for those you will impact for God's Kingdom.

3. Keep appropriate boundaries in your work and your relationships.

Life can easily get out of control. Our own dreams, desires, compulsions and emotional baggage, plus others' expectations and even abuse, can push us down a road we never intended to travel. The issue here is having proactive space or margin in our lives that will allow us to re-calibrate or heal when necessary. Sometimes the re-calibration involves dealing with emotional or relational issues, etc. before continuing on with career goals for instance. And like Job (in the Bible) for instance, sometimes life just flies off our course and all we can do is wait on God. But even when life feels out of control, we can still allow God to control our inner world as Job modeled. I can think of many friends who found themselves in crisis as a result of a lack of attention to their inner world and relationships. (As they have shared with me.)

It is significant that Paul mentions self-control as a fruit of the Spirit (Gal 5:22, 23). Peter also mentions it in his letter as part of his prescription for useful living. And when we talk about boundaries, we're talking about self-control. God knows we need to discern and choose between many options and temptations every day; this takes self-control. He's also given all believers the Holy Spirit to give us the power to choose self-control. The real issue here is if we will surrender to His Spirit in our times of choice. We must choose Spirit-led boundaries for ourselves and others so that we might reflect the lordship of Jesus and live out of a revitalized heart.

"One can have no smaller or greater mastery than mastery of oneself." -- *Leonardo da Vinci*[51]

Boundaries draw a line between where you will and will not go. These lines are not only moral lines (which God has drawn for us), but also personal lines in pursuit of authentic living—

living out God's plan for our lives. This means taking personal responsibility for our lives and choosing to live proactively on our path. It may mean saying no to an opportunity that looks good on one level (e.g., financially), but not so good at another (e.g., time spent away from family). Or it may mean settling for less in one area temporarily to attend to other needs.

In the book *Boundaries* by Doctors Henry Could and John Townsend, the authors comment, "The concept of boundaries comes from the very nature of God. God defines himself as a distinct, separate being and he is responsible for himself...God also limits what he will allow in his yard. He confronts sin and allows consequences for behavior. He guards his house and will not allow evil things to go on there. He invites people in who will love him, and he lets his love flow outward to them at the same time. The 'gates' of his boundaries open and close appropriately."

In the same way he gave us this "likeness" (Gen 1:26), he gave us personal responsibility within limits. He wants us to "rule and subdue" the Earth and to be responsible stewards over the life he has given us. To do that, we need to develop boundaries like God's."[52]

Jesus is our example in this as always. He often chose to leave a certain area even though there were good opportunities. He also didn't allow the accusations and traps set by religious leaders of the day to slow His accomplishment of the Father's will.

Living within your boundaries certainly takes daily wisdom and strength from God. Remember: There is nothing wrong with saying no to even good things. Remember too that when you say yes to one area of your life, you are saying no to another. The goal is to reflect Christ and His will in everything.

"Whoever says he abides in him (Jesus) ought to walk in the same way in he walked" (1 Jn 2:6).

4. Let God Define Your Success

"Come to me all who are weary and heavy laden and I will give you rest. Take my yoke upon you and learn from me, for I am gentle and lowly in

Sanity

heart and you will find rest for your souls. For my yoke is easy, and my burden is light." --Matt 11:28-30

When we're stressed out to the point of high anxiety, worry, fear and exhaustion, chances are we've lost sight of the significant goals in our life. We've begun to define success by what others think or by our own unhealthy ambitions. We can drive ourselves to reach a goal that God never intended for us.

You've probably heard the sayings, "Insanity is defined as doing the same thing over and over again expecting different results" and "If you aim at nothing, any road will get you there." Both of these thoughts demonstrate the extreme on both sides of living, either in aimlessness or compulsive drivenness. Both are wrong. We hurt ourselves and others in our wake when we lose sight of real success.

So how does God define success? He defines it by our faithfulness both to live (abide) in Christ and to do His will in the Holy Spirit's power. It means we derive our self-worth, our self-esteem and our being out of who we are in Christ and not by our fleshly desires or accomplishments. Author John Piper calls this "being satisfied with God." It means living with contentment in who we are in Him and who He is in us. We aren't looking to other people or things for our peace and contentment. This is the "being" side of our living.

Faithfulness also means we do His good and perfect will in His power. While we are content, it doesn't mean we are satisfied with the state of our world or complacent in our growth. It means we pursue God's vision for our future with joy and abandonment! It doesn't mean that we always understand what God is doing or that things will turn out as we've planned. But we can be certain that God is using it for His ultimate glory and our good. There is the unseen world that we are living for that some day will reveal the real picture, the real fruit and real rewards for our faithfulness.

The apostle Paul lived by this. At the end of his life he commented: *"I have fought the good fight, I have finished the race, I have kept the faith. Henceforth there is laid up for me the crown of righteousness, which the Lord, the righteous judge, will award to me that Day..."* Also, *"This slight momentary affliction is preparing for us an eternal weight of glory beyond all comparison..."* (2 Tim4:7, 2Cor4:17). And last, *"So now faith, hope, and love abide, these three; but the greatest of these is love..."* (1 Cor 13:13).

For us to avoid burnout in life we have to live by God's process. Paul expands on these principles in 2 Tim 2:3-6, 4:7:

"Share in suffering as a good soldier of Christ Jesus. No soldier gets entangled in civilian pursuits, since his aim is to please the one who enlisted him. An athlete is not crowned unless he competes according to the rules. It is the hard-working farmer who ought to have the first share of the crops. Think over what I say, for the Lord will give you understanding in everything." Here are some thoughts on these verses.

Paul calls us soldiers – fight the fight of faith!

We have a battle to fight. You are a soldier called to be strong, to put on the full armor and fight life's battles. Faith is a gift we've been given and it's the way we access grace to overcome (Eph 2:8, 6:16). It is by faith that we access God's power for living (Heb 11;6, 33). Be faithful to follow your Commander's direction and trust His wisdom. Are you taking up your armor and fighting by faith?

Paul calls us runners – Run the race of love!

We have a race to run; you are a runner. Run with endurance in mind. Strip off that which hinders and run in the way of love. Love is the course by which we run to show God to others as we also experience His love personally. God's mission in the world is a mission of love to meet the physical, emotional, relational and spiritual needs of people around you. If you don't run with love, you're not in God's race. Are you running in love first toward God then others?

Paul calls us farmers – Sow the seeds of hope!

We have hope to spread. You are a farmer; the harvest will come. Remember you're sowing seeds and in time you will see a harvest. We have a secure hope, a sure picture we've seen of the future; although dim, we know it is real. The hope we have is not just a wishing. New Testament hope refers to that which we know is true—that which will come to fruition. The more our minds are renewed, the more God's Spirit confirms in our hearts the reality of heaven and the joy of eternal life. Though it is mysterious and "we see in a mirror dimly," the reality of God's Kingdom becomes a bedrock by which we can live. And there will be a bountiful harvest beyond our wildest thoughts and dreams. Let that motivate you to keep sowing and watering seeds by your life, your words, your actions and your example. Are you sowing with the Gospel (good news), with patience and hope?

Now abide faith, hope and love...(1 Cor 13). Is there anything besides our salvation that is more important to understand and apply than God's definition of a successful life?

5. Live in grace – Never get over the Gospel!

Somewhere along the line we get the notion that once we accept Christ as our personal savior, i.e., the gospel, we then move on to a different level of life with God. We think now that we're saved, it's up to us to maintain our acceptance before God by our decisions. We put ourselves on a performance treadmill before God that places us under the burden of trying to produce a God glorifying life, with God's help.

The Authentic Musician

The problem with this is that we aren't supposed to try to live with God's help, but rather we're to let the Gospel have its full effect upon us so that we live as new creatures. We must believe and receive what the Gospel has done for us, to accept that the Gospel killed us (our old nature), buried us, raised us and seated us with Christ. And the life we now live is lived in freedom from condemnation (Rom 8), in newness of life (Rom 6), as a new creation (2 Cor5), and with a new heart (Ez 11:19), among many other blessings!

We are called to live in the contentment, joy and freedom of these truths by faith, always carrying the truth of the cross. That truth is our death and all that is sinful in us has been crucified with Christ. And it is the truth of the resurrection—our being raised to newness of life and peace with God. What pleases God is living in the truth of who we are in Christ and doing the works He's planned for us to do in His Spirit's power. I am already pleasing to Him in my person. From the point of my salvation on, it's my behavior that I must allow God to change and bring into alignment with His will.

It's easy for us to live as if what we're doing is so significant that we draw our self-worth from it or we feel the responsibility for fruitfulness in our life. We let this pressure steal the joy, peace and freedom we should be living in because of the Gospel. Perhaps this is why in Jesus' last discourse to the disciples, He reminded them that He was the vine and they were the branches. It's clear from this passage that we're to bear much fruit, fruit that will remain (Jn 15:8,16). The way of bearing fruit, however, is not by building bigger "branch muscles" of our own, trying to squeeze out as much life as we can. No, the branch simply receives life from the Vine and lets it show. It abides in the Vine. We must let the Vine do the nourishing and stretching. Jesus said, *"As the branch cannot bear fruit by itself, unless it abides in the vine, neither can you, unless you abide in me. I am the vine; you are the branches..."* (Jn 15:4).

Sanity

Abiding means we rest, live and accept all that Jesus has done and says we are in Him. It means we cease trying to create our own life (flesh) and we receive the life of the Vine, obeying all our Vine says we are to do, trusting Him to bear fruit through us.

Author Larry Crabb put it this way, "If we build on the first foundation, the flesh, our core passion will be for blessings, whichever ones we value most. And our core experience, beneath whatever else we feel, will be pressure, the pressure to live a certain way to get the life we want."

"If we build on the second foundation, the Spirit, our core passion will be for God, to know Him and honor Him in any circumstance. And our core experience will be freedom, the freedom to draw near to God across a bridge we neither constructed nor maintain. And in that freedom we'll discover both the passion to live well and with wisdom to know what that means."[53]

Pressure or freedom—which is your experience? It takes a lifetime to really unpack and release our baggage that beckons us to live under pressure. But, it is the Gospel (the bridge) that releases us and heals us and gives us the freedom to live in the Spirit, abide in the Vine. Such news is beyond our wildest dreams, isn't it? Authentic Christian lives are built on the Spirit. We can increasingly reflect the true life of Christ in us, uniquely displaying the glory for which He has created us, all for His glory. What an incredible adventure—much more than just sanity!

"But the fruit of the Spirit is love, joy, peace, patience, kindness, goodness, faithfulness, gentleness and self-control...if we live by the Spirit, let us also walk by the Spirit" (Gal 5:22,25).

Oh, how I hope you experience this life of the heart each day and that it is reflected in your art. Our authentic God loves you and me too much to leave us in surface-only living.

You can maintain sanity and grow in authenticity by:

- Connecting with God daily
- Connecting with other believers regularly
- Keeping appropriate boundaries in your work and your relationships.
- Letting God define your success
- Living in grace, never getting over the Gospel!

Follow-up Questions

Chapter 9: Sanity

1. What disciplines do you need to regularly implement to realign your heart – to listen to your heart and to God?

2. What changes can you make in your environment or schedule to live in authentic community and mentoring relationships?

3. Are you quick to deal with unhealthy relationships and influences?

4. Do you have a personal definition of success for your day as well as your life work? Is it the same as God's?

5. Do you continue to be amazed at the impact of the Gospel on your life and others? If not, take some time to reflect and listen to people's life change stories!

The Authentic Musician

10. Leaving an Authentic Trail

"Do you see what this means-all these pioneers who blazed the way, all these veterans cheering us on? It means we better get on with it. Strip down, start running-and never quit!" (Heb12:1,2 MSB)

If you've ever done any backpacking or hiking through the woods, you know how helpful another's trail can be to navigate rough or even dangerous terrain. The older I get, the more aware I am of what my life might be speaking to others. This is probably no more apparent to me than as a parent, but certainly many others are onlookers. People look to you for inspiration, wisdom, strength and beauty whether you know it or not. Do we not also look to other people, especially authentic people for this? And ultimately, the One looking at us is Jesus, our example and the author of our faith (Heb 12:1-3).

The challenge is this: How we can live today, and tomorrow, authentically? How can we leave a trail worth following, one that won't lead others in the wrong direction, or worse, *off a cliff?* I'm talking about longevity, endurance and persistence.

The Authentic Musician

A Trailblazer Speaks

Imagine you lived to be 120 years old and you saw a whole generation and more pass before your eyes... a generation of more than a million people! You've seen the consequences of good and bad decisions, yours as well as a multitude of others'. You've seen God intervene many times in your life. If you could tell the next generation something, what would it be? What do you think you would have learned?

The fact that you lived to share your experience of over 120 years would guarantee that you had something to say and that others would most likely listen. What would people ask you? What do you think you would say? Would it have any bearing on being an authentic musician or artist?

There was once such a man, and he was a musician, though he only wrote one song of which we know. He lived 120 years, and at the end he wrote of his conclusions about life. What he wrote answers many of our questions.

The man was Moses, and he recorded in Psalm 90 his thoughts for future generations. His concern was helping us see what really matters in life. We could title this Psalm: *What really matters in life.*

Moses starts his thoughts with that which is not bound by time or space—he starts with God. *"Lord, you have been our dwelling place in all generations. Before the mountains were brought forth, or ever you had formed the earth and the world, from everlasting to everlasting you are God"* (Psalm 90:1,2).

Life starts and ends with God. God had taught Moses that He is eternal; from eternity past to eternity future, He has and will exist. He operates outside of time. He is also present, for his people. He is their dwelling place—the place of life, the place of significance, the place of purpose and peace.

Leaving an Authentic Trail

In contrast, Moses moves from God to man and the fact that we are temporal, transient, and our days on Earth are few. *"You return man to dust and say, 'Return, O children of man!' for a thousand years in your sight are but as yesterday when it is past, or as a watch in the night. You sweep them away as with a flood; they are like a dream, like grass that is renewed in the morning; in the morning it flourishes and is renewed; in the evening it fades and withers"* (Psalm 90, 3-6).

Moses saw birth, life and death every day up close and personal. Unlike we do in our sanitized, media-focused world, he walked among his people in real life and came to realize how fleeting and sometimes mysterious our lives are: *"For we are brought to an end by your anger; by your wrath we are dismayed. You have set our iniquities before you, our secret sins in the light of your presence. For all our days pass away under your wrath; we bring our years to an end like a sigh. The years of our life are seventy, or even by reason of strength eighty; yet their span is but toil and trouble; they are soon gone, and we fly away"* (Psalm 90,.7-10).

Moses is trying to bring some perspective to us here. Our lives are short. Oh, how badly we need to remember that! We're prone to think of only the here and now. Though Jesus has taken God's wrath for us on the cross, we still live in a world sentenced to terminate and we live in bodies that will eventually die. Soon we will fly away! Elsewhere, the apostle James says our lives are like a vapor or a breath. Think of it! Your life is just like your last breath, the one you just took. It's gone before you know it!

From here Moses asks a question, *"Who considers the power of your anger, and your wrath according to the fear of you* (v.11)? We might expand on this verse to say, "Who considers all that God has revealed to us?" This is a rhetorical question and perhaps the response is that few people truly consider deeply what God has revealed to man. God's revelation through His Word and His Spirit are critical to our endurance and victory in this life. It is through constant "truth injections" into our hearts from His Word and His intimate presence that He nourishes, heals and restores our hearts. Taking the time and space necessary to absorb this is critical. Is it in your schedule?

"So teach us to number our days that we may get a heart of wisdom" (v.12). Life is lived one day at a time, not one month, year or decade. Seizing our day in a heart-building way is crucial to our authenticity. Don't put off communing with God till next Sunday or Christmas. It must happen each day.

"Return, O Lord! How long? Have pity on your servants! Satisfy us in the morning with your steadfast love that we may rejoice and be glad all our days. Make us glad for as many days as you have afflicted us, and for as many years as we have seen evil" (v.13-15). We long for the future day of Christ's return. That's our ultimate dream and sure hope. But in the meantime, may His presence satisfy us... that we may rejoice and be glad. Take time each day to receive God's love and dwell in His presence to ensure you will "be glad" all your days. This isn't an option. The apostle Jude says, *"But you, beloved, build yourselves up in your most holy faith; pray in the Holy Spirit; keep yourselves in the love of God, waiting for the mercy of our Lord Jesus Christ that leads to eternal life"* (Jude 20,21). John Piper says in *Future Grace:* "God is most glorified in us when we are most satisfied in Him." Being satisfied with God means we're making our ways His ways, and our paths His path, and He is our first desire and want.

"Let your work be shown to your servants, and your glorious power to their children. Let the favor of the Lord our God be upon us, and establish the work of our hands upon us; yes, establish the work of our hands" (v. 16-17)! Discerning God's mission for our lives is crucial to our ultimate satisfaction. It was Jesus' relationship with the Father and His convictions that propelled Him to endure the cross. Hebrews 12:2 tells us that He was looking forward to the joy that was on the other side of the cross—and

the dream of the Father's presence, along with our fellowship! That should be our ultimate dream, too, along with smaller dreams He places on our hearts.

Jesus demonstrated that His life was about doing the Father's will (Jn 5:19). He was able through disciplined listening and prayer to know what was next on the Father's adventure for His life. Then by God's power, He walked in obedience to the Father. The same should be true for us. This doesn't mean life will always make sense, nor will it always be comfortable. But the joy of obedience does not compare to anything else, according to Jesus (Luke 18:29,30).

So, what is Moses' bottom line in this Psalm? All of this points to the hard work of guarding and growing our hearts each day. The battle is real, and in terms of longevity there is no other way to be successful our whole lives. We must guard our hearts!

Moses certainly left a good trail, but the record of people in the Bible who finished strong is actually quite dismal. This is especially true in the Old Testament. People who experienced a measure of success seemed to always get side tracked and pulled away from living a faithful life. The New Testament church shows a different side to this. Once believers experienced the redeemed life in Christ and the filling of His Spirit, they lived in a way that often confounded the people around them and "turned the world upside down." Their witness was unstoppable, and even though we know there have been hypocrites, imposters and failures since then, still the church has survived to the current day.

Leaving a good trail involves, first of all, *making* a good trail, and second, *marking* it as you go so others can follow. But we have to ask, what has happened? History both past and recent shows that many of us Christians are not leaving a good trail to follow. So many of us have failed to be salt and light in our culture. Instead of being the fragrance of Christ, we've been a source of disgust or even reproach to the name of Christ! So many struggle to make a good or authentic trail over the long haul but fail. What can we do? Does Moses' Psalm and the rest of God's Word have anything to say? Yes, it does! Here are a few thoughts to ponder.

Some Keys to Authentic Longevity

First, *live one day at a time.* Psalm 90 reminds us to number our days—not months or years. Likewise Jesus said, *"Do not be anxious about tomorrow, for tomorrow will be anxious for itself. Sufficient for the day is its own trouble."* In other words, trust tomorrow to the Lord and focus on His grace for today. You can't fight tomorrow's battles today. Part of today's battle may be preparing and planning for tomorrow's battles, but what you do today for His glory is what counts! Like Psalm 90, James 4:13-16 warns and reminds us that tomorrow isn't guaranteed; our life is a vapor. So let's glorify God by receiving His blessings and fighting His battles and realizing He's big enough to handle tomorrow.

Second, *keep a right view of God*—who He is. The most important thing about any man is his view of God. Bill Bright was a great man of faith and founder of one of the largest ministries in the world, Campus Crusade for Christ. He writes, "Everything about our lives—our attitudes, motives, desires, actions, and even our words—is influenced by our view of God." [54]

Third, *let God speak to your heart about what is real and what is eternal.* Before losing the race, we lose heart. Before we quit fighting, we lose heart. Losing heart is the chief disease behind inauthenticity. Keeping a close eye on your heart is essential for your success. In Christ we've received a new heart, and God's plan for us is to discover and live from it! (See *Waking the Dead*, John Eldredge.) For artists, losing heart is probably the main reason we give up on our creativity or growth. Our heart is the seat of our deepest emotions and our deepest thoughts. It is where the real you dwells. When we lose heart, we live from the surface and fail to prioritize and listen to what our heart and God's spirit are telling us.

Fourth, *let God show you your path*. He has a great plan for each one of us in every area of our lives. His grace meets us at every turn. When we fail, being authentic demands that we confess and turn from our failure. Does this mean that we have to work our way back to Him? No, in His mercy and grace He meets us where we are and continues to work with us from the place we are—as long as we turn back to Him. When we successfully do His will, we rejoice and humbly seek His presence and look for His next assignment. In Psalm 32:8 God says, *"I will instruct you and teach you in the way you should go; I will counsel you with my eye upon you."*

Fifth, *prioritize Jesus as your first love*. This is close to living from your heart, but speaks to the deepest reason for our lack of obedience and endurance. God wants a relationship with us that affects our works. In fact, He wants our relationship with Him to take priority. Revelation 3 tells us that even though the Ephesians had done wonderful works in His name, they were displeasing to Him because they abandoned their first love in the process. This is relevant to us today. We can become so absorbed in our work or other relationships that our intimacy with Christ takes lower priority. This is just what the enemy (Satan) likes. Inauthenticity then begins to seep out in our attitudes, ambitions and actions, thus tarnishing our witness and strength. Your work then becomes driven by:

Duty rather than *joy*

Fear rather than *love*

Selfishness rather than *servanthood*

Doubt rather than *faith*

If knowing, enjoying and celebrating Jesus isn't our first desire, then our desires are off; we're living from the flesh rather than the new life of the Spirit (Rom 7:6). The flesh operates by rules: "If, then"—i.e, if I do this, then God will do that and I will get what I really want (which isn't God). The flesh tries to substitute other people or things for God. The life of the Spirit however operates by relationship: we receive love and give God love-motivated obedience. Our new nature delights most in knowing God, not getting from God (Larry Crabb's book, *The Pressure's Off*, develops this idea).

Keys to Artistic Longevity

On the artistic side of things, what will keep you going through the long haul?

First, *personal discipline*—i.e., who you are when no one's looking. *"The pain of discipline costs much less than the pain of regret"* (unknown).

Discipline is a hard word for many of us. Even seeing the word can bring up negative feelings. It reminds me that life and artistic creation is a battle...and the battle is real whether I want to admit it or not! If you're intent on living authentically, you're in for a battle. As an artist, becoming who God has created you to be and doing His will mustn't be diminished to just "getting by and living comfortably."

There's no substitute for personal discipline, both to maintain your artistic skill and to grow further. In our culture today more than perhaps ever, there are so many distractions that can pull us away from the decisions, commitments, persistence and rewards of personal discipline. It reminds me of Jesus' words about this battle we face, *"The thief comes only to steal, kill and destroy. I came that they might have life and have it abundantly"* (Jn 10:10). This speaks to every area of our lives including God's design for your artistic development. Make growth a lifestyle.

Leaving an Authentic Trail

One key to developing this kind of discipline is to develop your vision. When you lack motivation, it's time to gain a relevant vision for your work. Take seriously who or from what you get your motivation or vision. What would happen in our world if Christian artists took their heart and skill development seriously? Think how much more beauty there would be in the Earth, how much more redemption there would be in our culture, and even how many more people would experience salvation! We've seen from history how the arts were transformed and in many ways set free in the reformations of the 16th and 17th centuries. As artists began to understand God's word better, many advancements in creative expression and cultural impact through the arts were born. None of that would have happened if artists had not developed their skills (and heart) through personal discipline over the long haul. We have the same opportunity in our slice of time on this earth.

A second way to develop discipline is *living in community* with other artists Notice there quotes:

. *"I value the friend who for me finds time on his calendar, but I cherish the friend who for me does not consult the calendar" (Robert Brault).*[55]

"Friendship is unnecessary, like philosophy, like art... It has no survival value; rather it is one of those things that give value to survival"

(C. S. Lewis).

"The friend who can be silent with us in a moment of despair or confusion, who can stay with us in an hour of grief and bereavement, who can tolerate not knowing, not curing, not healing and face with us the reality of our powerlessness, that is a friend who cares" (Henri Nouwen).

This principle may be obvious to us, but it is not always easy to practice. Besides being a principle for our heart health, it's also true emotionally and artistically. As much as people may think artist are "lone rangers," anti-social or just not gregarious, when these artists emerge from the creative process, they need community. It's just a fact of how we are created. Authentic community can re-inspire the artistic heart. I hope you can see this point as a blessing and a warning. Resources are available through online websites and media to keep us aware of greater heights we can pursue artistically, but there is no substitute for real people having input into our lives.

A third way to develop discipline is by *keeping the bigger picture in mind*. It's the artist's life body of work that speaks for him. Study other artists' lives, especially those whose works are lasting beyond their own lifetime. So many of the greatest classical composers were not recognized as such during their lifetimes. What if they had given up 10 or 30 years before their death? As Christians, we have the added incentive that we are to live from and for eternity. So, keep producing. Francis Schaeffer's comments bear repeating here:

"The artist makes a body of work and this body of work shows his worldview. No one, for example, who understands Michelangelo or Leonardo, can look at their work without understanding something of their respective worldviews. Nonetheless, these artists began by making works of art, and then their worldviews showed through the body of their work. I emphasize the body of an artist's work because it is impossible for any single painting, for example, to reflect the totality of an artist's view of reality. But when we see a collection of an artist's paintings or a series of a poet's poems or a number of a novelist's novels, both the outline and some of the details of the artist's conception of life shine through. [56]

Leaving an Authentic Trail

As you grow older, is it not true that you will learn new lessons and your worldview will continue to change? Should not the world benefit from your discovery of who you are, who God is, and His love through your art? Again, carpe diem!

Fourth, build discipline in your life by *making it about other people; be connected to a worthy cause.* Do you realize that your gifts are meant to be used for the "common good" as well as your own encouragement? For me, nothing compares with knowing my gifts are being used to influence people and the world for good. Author Bill Hybels says we've each been given a "holy discontent"[57]—something we see in the world that we can't stand to let pass. He contends that God has particular needs He wants us to be passionate about changing in the world... and we can play a part in it.

Causes that are significant are always ultimately about people because God is all about people. And He more than likely will compel you to engage with others in a common cause. Our art can be used greatly to encourage co-laborers and to ignite them to action.

Bono of U2 is a great example of this these days. He uses his platform and his writing to bring attention to the plight of AIDS and poverty in Africa, among other things.[58]

A key to making it about other people is to be exposed to the needs of others. Your heart won't break for others with whom you have no connection. Take advantage of opportunities to personally get close to people and their needs, and you will find God burdening your heart. It may range from world relief to community awareness, from meeting physical needs to meeting spiritual needs. *Whatever you find yourself becoming burdened by, let your art in on it!* As we've discovered earlier: The arts are valuable gifts from God for the expression of our hearts, *the encouragement of others* and the pleasure of God. Having a cause beyond ourselves can keep us creating for our entire lives.

Fifth, *create balance* to build discipline. Life is a balancing act. There is a season for everything and as we go to and from varying circumstances, there are times for intense creativity and times for focusing on other things in life. We are to be stewards of all we've been given, and our ultimate audience is God. Living authentically demands that we put first things first (our relationship with God) and give our gifts attention in their time and place. The danger, of course, is that we go to the extreme of either making our art too important or not important enough in our lives, even abandoning it. If you find yourself abandoning your artistic giftedness (or know other who have), you must ask if God has made it clear you are to do so. After all, your stewardship is to Him.

Besides this, it's important to recognize that living with balance, boundaries and a Sabbath rest is the way of life God prescribes. Creative expression is work, and it can be very draining. This demands that we find legitimate recovery, refreshment and encouragement to keep moving forward.

Thoughts on Marking your Trail

When we hike through the woods, we have to think continually about how we're going to make our way home and how others can follow us without getting hurt or lost. Our path can either lead others astray or save them from wrong turns if we mark our trail well. What are some ways we can mark the way for others?

First of all, *be intentional about impacting others.* If you're making a good trail, you will impact others. Our example is hugely powerful. Paul knew this and was confident in saying, *"Follow me as I follow Christ."* He was telling others, "Here's a sign post; Christ is my leader!" But realize that it is others—your closest friends and family—who are your "letter" to the world. In 2 Corinthians 2:2,3 Paul proclaims that it's the changed lives of the Corinthians that are his proof to the world of his ministry. He left a trail thick with impacted, changed lives as he shared the Gospel. Your impact on people, your relationships, are the ultimate signposts of your path.

Second, your *authenticity and personal integrity* are markers, too. This gets down to decisions you make in how your treat others and how you spend your time, energy and resources. Prayer is probably one of the least recognized markers. In heaven, however, I suspect we'll be amazed at the impact our prayers had on people's lives and circumstances. Obviously, this affects your relational impact, too.

Third, *your works or your art are markers*, and in some cases, these markers outlive other markers, though rarely. This can take the form of writings, journaling, blogging, and other creative works that can impact your audience. Likewise, the service we do in Jesus' name is also a marker. Remember His words at the judgment: *"Truly, I say to you, as you did it* (or did not do it—minister to the hungry, thirsty, naked, sick or imprisoned) *to one of the least of these my brothers, you did* (or did not do it) *to me"* (my paraphrase) Matthew 25:31-45.

Who's the trail really for?

This brings us to the ultimate "follower" of our trail. Certainly, we want our trail to show the way for others to move forward. I'm so thankful for those who have gone ahead of me, and continue to show the way. Even the Bible characters themselves are meant to be trail markers for us (1 Cor 10:6, Heb 12:1). But the previous verses in Matthew 25 point to another audience, our ultimate audience: Jesus! He is following us! Not in the sense of imitating us but of observing us. He's cheering us on to run the race and to mark our path well. There's no condemnation for us as his children, but He's intensely interested in our works, our ambitions, attitudes and actions. We wants us to hike or run with endurance and with no hindrances or entanglements (Heb 12:1,2)! Oh, may we continue to grow and be "steadfast, immovable, always abounding in the work of the Lord, knowing that our labor in the Lord is not in vain" (1 Cor 15:58).

So, how can you be an authentic musician, artist or leader to your last breath? How can you leave an authentic trail? It all gets back to God's favor, His grace. His grace is on you if you've received Christ. The opportunity is yours and mine each day to choose to live by His grace and authentically leave the world a better place. Let us seize each day for His glory!

Let the favor of the Lord our God be upon us, and establish the work of our hands upon us; yes, establish the work of our hands! (Psalm90:17)

Follow-up Questions

Chapter 10: Leaving An Authentic Trail

1. Are longevity and endurance desires of yours? Do you recognize that it will be a battle?

2. Of the five points under Authentic Longevity, which are most pressing to you these days?

3. Of the five points under Artistic Longevity, which are most pressing to you these days?

4. Hebrews 12:1,2 encourages us to lay aside every encumbrance and the sin, which so easily entangles us, and to run with endurance the race marked out for us. What are some encumbrances and entanglements you struggle with and how are you dealing with them? What would running with endurance look like for you these days? Are you on the right trail? Should you seek help so you can leave a better trail?

The Authentic Musician

11. Postlude

Picture thousands of gifted artists and musicians everywhere living transformed lives, using their gifts in every strata of society to express their hearts, building up people while bringing the love and truth of Christ, and ultimately glorifying God. What a powerful sense of purpose and significance they experience as they live out their created purpose!

I'm not talking about stuffy, churchy, mediocre musicians and artists. I'm talking about authentic musicians engaged in the greatest cause, mission and challenge of all time—that of bringing His Kingdom to Earth ... fulfilling His commission to help bring new life to people in every culture, nation and tongue. That of being salt and light in the world. That of making disciples of every nation. And that of building believers who passionately worship God in spirit and truth. I'm talking about artists influencing their culture through excellent, relevant, creative and truth-revealing art.

My first major trip out of the U.S. was to Hong Kong and the Philippines with a music team missions trip. I will never forget my feelings as a young man when I came back to the U.S. and began to realize the immensity of the world and its needs physically, and especially spiritually. I was captured by the sense of urgency, purpose and mission God had me on. I also looked at my life trajectory and that of other musicians I knew, and realized that in some ways we were living in a system or worldview that was totally ignorant of the opportunities to use our gifts to help change the world.

Most of us musicians wanted nothing more than a comfortable and fun life. Others of us sought the goal of trying to build our own kingdom of influence and affluence we hoped success in the music industry would bring. And now, looking back after 30 years, it's astonishing to realize that very few musicians in my generation have pursued authentic living, let alone using their music in significant ways—ways that reflect our real purpose. Many are suffering relationally, creatively and spiritually. Others like myself who heard and followed God's way, though imperfectly, can attest that there is no other life worth living. My longing is for others like you to experience this and much more!

Life trajectory is an interesting thing. It's part of what makes us human—the ability to choose the direction our lives will take. Regardless of what your life trajectory has been, you can choose to change it. You can choose to make changes that will move you toward the life for which you were created. You can choose to let God work in your life and help you discover your new heart, your gifts, talents and calling from this point forward. You can choose to live authentically rather than in hypocrisy or in denial of the truth.

As an artist, you can choose to let the Creator Himself infuse your heart with new life and creativity. You can surrender to His work of transforming your life so you can help transform others. God is looking for authentic artists who are available and obedient to Him to help transform cultures, reach the lost, and build His body, the church.

He is looking for authentic artists—people who know their giftedness, develop their skill, and create art with a "spiritually alive" heart.

Postlude

Who understand that the arts are valuable gifts from God for the expression of our hearts, the encouragement of others and the pleasure of God.

It is my hope that these chapters have helped you capture the Spirit's call to your heart. No one loves you more; no one has a better calling for you. May you and I continue to listen and be transformed into all that our redemption in Christ has given us. To God be all glory!

Now may you be filled with the knowledge of His will with all spiritual wisdom and understanding so that you may walk in a manner worthy of the Lord, to please Him in all respects, bearing fruit in every good work, increasing in the knowledge of God, being strengthened with power according to his glorious might, for the attaining of all steadfastness with patience, joyously giving thanks to him who has qualified us to share in the inheritance of the saints in light. (Col 1:9-12)

Appendix

The Authentic Musician

Believing in God and Beginning a Relationship

The importance of your beliefs

Everyone has beliefs; it's part of being human. It's easy to never really face the questions of God and life, and to just accept without serious consideration what we've grown up with or been told. But these issues are extremely important, and we must evaluate and adjust our beliefs when needed. Ultimately, your beliefs direct your life. A belief is not just an intellectual assent that something is true. Intellectual assent starts and stays in our head; beliefs, however, start in our head but move to our heart where we decide, by our will, to accept something as true or not. Beliefs determine our worldview. Your beliefs provide the basis by which you make all of your significant decisions and actions in life.

In fact, our core beliefs are the foundation of *all* we say and do. Our ambitions, attitudes and actions reflect what we really believe about ourselves, others and our circumstances. We can become masters of appearing on the outside something different than what we believe on the inside, at least for a while. But ultimately the truth comes out. How often do we see people professing to believe something, but once we look closely at their lives or hear their words, find it is clear no such belief exists? That's called hypocrisy or "mask wearing." We also often find it easy to accuse others of this, but fail see it in our own lives.

Do you know what you believe about the basic questions of life and why? It may be that your beliefs are faulty or you're building your beliefs on a lie. That was Eve's problem in the Garden of Eden. She accepted the lie Satan told her: "You shall surely not die!" Satan knew that if he could get her to change her beliefs or make her doubt God's truth, she would begin to serve his (Satan's) purposes rather than God's. Conversely, the apostle John writes that his main purpose for writing his Gospel was that we would believe that Jesus was the Messiah and find life (Jn 20:31). He knew too that what we choose to believe strikes at the core of our person and potential.

We can't talk about having an authentic heart without listening to what our Creator says about it. Only the Creator knows the real purpose for his creation. Only God knows the real reason and unique purpose for which He created you! He is willing to speak to you, but first you need to settle some basic questions about who God is and what He's done if you hope to have a relationship with Him and discover your heart.

Two basic questions everyone must grapple with are, Is He real? and, Has He revealed truth to us? (or, Has He spoken to us?). Having a sufficient answer for these questions lays the foundation for further answers and discoveries. *"Everyone that comes to God must believe that He exists and rewards those who seek Him"* (Heb 11:6).

Basic Belief #1 – God is Real

While I won't try to prove God exists, I will say there is more evidence to believe there *is* a God than to believe there is not. It takes much more "faith" to deny the road signs of his existence through creation, history and our conscience than to believe in His non-existence.

176

Furthermore, the weight of evidence for believing in God and specifically the God of the Bible is overwhelming from a historical and intellectual viewpoint. It still takes faith but not a blind, unsupportable faith. Here are some general arguments for you to consider. I also encourage you to read the books referenced at the end of this section.

Some road signs pointing to God's existence:

- Creation – To look at the complexity, creativity and mystery of our universe from macro- and micro-perspectives points to an intelligent Designer. From the smallest molecule to the largest star, the simplest life form to human life, all point to a Creator God.

- The Bible – The Bible is miraculous in its predictions about future events that have taken place. Plus, the consistency and yet variety of its authors points to the ultimate author, God Himself. It claims to be God's revelation of Himself to humankind and has millions of witnesses throughout history who point to its inspiration.

- Jesus Christ's life and resurrection – Christianity's claim is that Jesus Himself was God in human flesh. There is historical evidence to believe that Jesus lived, died and rose from the dead. Based on historical evidence and witnesses, we can believe in Jesus' resurrection as surely as the fact that George Washington lived and died, or any other person from recent history. By his resurrection Jesus proved He was God as He claimed, and He has shown us who God is.

- Other Religions – What about the other religions that claim to present the truth about God, or gods? All other religions are based on individuals' writings from their own inspiration or insight. All other religions present a way to work our way to God by our actions or good works. Christianity is unique in that it is based not

177

on a teacher whose body lays today in a grave somewhere, but on a teacher who rose from the dead to prove His deity, truth and love for us. Getting to God is not a matter of works, but of accepting His gift of salvation through Christ. According to the Bible, all roads do not lead to God, because God's road is a person who is the Truth (John14:6), who has moral absolutes and unique attributes that do not change. He is loving and holy and by definition cannot accept that which is not loving or holy. All religions do not lead to God, but for the person who truly continues to seek God, I believe their journey will eventually lead to Jesus Christ and, through Him, to God.

There are also many intellectual arguments for believing in the existence of God. They range from a philosophical to scientific perspective.

- The *first cause* argument (or "cosmological argument") takes the existence of the universe to entail the existence of a being that created it. It does so based on the fact that the universe had a beginning. There must, the first cause argument says, be something that caused that beginning, a first cause of the universe.

- The argument from *design* focuses on the fact that the universe is fit for human habitation. There are many possibilities for how the universe might have been—it might have had different laws of physics; it might have had a different arrangement of planets and stars; it might have begun with a bigger or a smaller big bang—and the vast majority of these universes would not have allowed for the existence of life. We are very fortunate indeed to have a universe that does.

- The *moral* argument appeals to the existence of moral laws as evidence of God's existence. According to this argument, there couldn't be such a thing as morality without God. To use the words that Sartre attributed to Dostoyevsky, "If there is no God, then everything is permissible." That there are moral laws, then, that not everything is impermissible, proves that God exists.[59] (Other suggested readings: *The Case for Faith,* Lee Strobel; *Evidence that Demands a Verdict* and *More than a Carpenter*, Josh McDowell.)

Author Josh McDowell states, "Is there truly a God? How can anyone be sure such a being exists? We believe that questions relating to the existence of God can be intelligently answered. The reason we know God exists is that He has told us so, and He has revealed Himself to us. He has told us all about who He is, what He is like and what His plan is for planet earth. He has revealed these things to mankind through the Bible."[60]

"Atheism turns out to be too simple," says author C.S. Lewis. "If the whole universe has no meaning, we should never have found out that it has no meaning...Now that I am a Christian I do not have moods in which the whole thing looks very improbable: but when I was an atheist I had moods in which Christianity looked terribly probable" (*Mere Christianity*).[61]

Basic Belief #2 – God has revealed truth to us

There is ample evidence to believe that God not only does exist but that He has communicated to us through creation and the Bible. Jesus himself validated the Bible. Why should we believe Jesus? Because He proved his validity, authority and deity by his resurrection. No other religious leader has risen from the dead. Why should we believe the Bible? Ultimately because Jesus said it is the word of God.

Has God revealed all truth? No. In fact, there is much He has left for us to discover and much that will always be a mystery or hidden from us

179

(Deut 29:29). The Bible is extremely clear on certain essential subjects and less clear on others non-essentials (see endnote in Chapter 3). But we can trust that what He has revealed is reliable because it came from God Himself, who is trustworthy and never changes.

What are the implications of these two beliefs? They are huge, as you may guess. The promises and truths of the Bible provide an amazing context for us to live our lives, experience new life and discover our heart. It promises power for today's challenges and an eternity in heaven.

According to the Bible, what you believe ultimately provides the tracks run on either toward life or death. We are finite creatures, we are limited. We don't have all the answers and we must be humble enough to seek real answers from God to our deepest questions and needs. As we seek God, the Bible says He will reveal Himself to us. He will show us His desire for us to move from living with a natural, broken heart to a new, redeemed heart. The differences in right and wrong beliefs can be pictured like this.

Wrong Beliefs:

- Lead to death
- Are based on half-truths or lies
- Lead to frustration and discord
- Lead to more deception
- Lead to darkness and bondage to self-destructive living.
- May seem natural, reasonable and esay to believe

Believing in God and Beginning a Relationship

> **Right Beliefs** (according to the Bible)
>
> - Lead to life
> - Are based on truth
> - Lead to peace and satisfaction
> - Lead to greater understanding of God, ourselves and the world
> - Lead to light and freedom to discover the real heart Christ died to give us.
> - May be counter-cultural and lead to sacrifice

As I'm sure you can tell by now, I am convinced that these two basic beliefs are trustworthy and I seek to live my life by them. The Bible indeed is the source of truth and that the God of the Bible is real.

What difference has this made for me? When I graduated from college, I had to decide what I was going to do with my life. At that time I had been challenged to think based on these two truths: that God is real and His word is true. This provided a "world view" for me to evaluate the opportunities I had as well my values concerning people, money, music, education and the role spiritual growth should play in my life. I'm not saying it made my decision process easier, but it made me think beyond just how much money or fame I could earn to more significant issues like helping people and building significant relationships.

Accepting just these two beliefs is *not* a minor thing. In fact, the implications of believing God and His word are very far reaching and it is often a long process for some to understand and embrace them personally. Let me encourage you that if you are having difficulty accepting these beliefs, do not give up on the process. Ask God to reveal

Himself and His truth to you and be attentive. Don't just settle for believing what others tell you or what your family raised you to believe. God wants you to seek Him personally and to have your own personal convictions. He longs for you to discover the abundant life He created you for!

If you accept these two beliefs—that God is real and He has revealed truth to us through the Bible—then the next question as we look at being authentic is, What does He have to say about me? His answer to that is to look at what He says about our heart. Our heart is what defines who we really are.

What about the heart?

The first discovery as we look at the Bible is that our hearts are mysterious, and there are often forces at work in our hearts that pull us in different directions. We can feel the pull sometimes to good things and oftentimes to bad things. This is especially true if we look inside our hearts to our motives. Our motives are often hard to discern or may be multilayered, but if we're honest we'll often see a *bent* that puts ourselves first and above all others. When we choose to live this way, it can result in harm to our relationships and ourselves. The reason for this bent as the Bible describes it, is that we are born into a fallen world, with a fallen nature. The Bible says it is our very nature since the fall of man to choose *ourselves* and *our way* above all else. In this world, we're born as inauthentic people.

This wasn't the original intent of God for our hearts. It wasn't what we were designed for, but because of the choice to live independently of God and his plan, we became alienated from Him. In fact, the Bible says our spirits are deadened and our hearts are sick. Unless we enter into the "redeemed life" God offers us, we will continue to live alienated from Him and unable to live in the authenticity and adventure for which we were created.

The Bible pictures it like this:

Pre-fall: (life in the garden of Eden)	The fall of man	Post-fall: (life in the "world system")
• Perfect body		• Mortal Imperfect body
• Perfect relationships		• Imperfect relationships
• Harmony with nature and fullfillment in work		• Frustration in nature and work
• Alive spiritually		• Dead spiritually
• Unlimited potential in the use of our gifts and talents for noble purposes. • Peace and wholeness		• Use of our gifts and talent focused on self gratification • Void and emptiness
• Good heart		• Desperate heart
• Eternal life with God		• Eternal separation
• Free will		• Free will by enslaved to sin
• Significance from our relaitonship with God		• Significance drawn from our position

timeline

Notice that life in a "post-fall" world is a formula for inauthentic living. When someone strays from being who they were created to be and doing what they were created to do, they become inauthentic or counterfeit *reflections* of their original identity and purpose. We each were originally created in God's mind for a specific purpose and calling.

But, due to our birth into a fallen world and state, we are unable to really fulfill our purpose.

In a post-fall world we are cut off from a relationship with God, and in our other relationships our life often becomes a series of masks we wear to cover up our failures and our brokenness.

So, we not only live inauthentic lives, but hypocritical lives void of an intimate relationship with God (for which we were created), and frustrated in our work and other relationships.

Without a radical intervention, we are stuck in the web of inauthenticity, either settling for mediocrity or addicted to something we think will fill the void in our lives. We are dead spiritually and living with broken hearts. What will deliver us from life in this post-fall world? Will money, sex, power, technology, adventure, human relationships or fame provide the real life we were created for? Jimi Hendrix, who likely died of a drug overdose said, "Music is my religion"[62] Is music the answer? Perhaps this U2 song sums it up best, which describes the search we all are on, whether believers or not. The difference for the believers, however, is that we have tasted what we're looking for and, having tasted, we know there's more and where to find it.

> I have climbed highest mountains
> I have run through the fields
> Only to be with you
> Only to be with you
> I have run
> I have crawled
> I have scaled these city walls
> These city walls
> Only to be with you

Believing in God and Beginning a Relationship

But I still haven't found what I'm looking for
But I still haven't found what I'm looking for

I have kissed honey lips
Felt the healing fingertips
It burned like a fire
This burning desire
I have spoke with the tongues of angels
I have held the hand of a devil
It was warm in the night
I was cold as a stone

But I still haven't found what I'm looking for
But I still haven't found what I'm looking for

I believe in the Kingdom Come
When all the colors will bleed into one
Bleed into one
Well, yes I'm still running
You broke the bonds
And you loosened the chains
Carried the cross
Of all my shame
all my shame
You know I believe it

But I still haven't found what I'm looking for
But I still haven't found what I'm looking for
But I still haven't found what I'm looking for

Hope for desperate lives

How do we escape from living with a broken heart? How do we discover and begin to live the adventure for which we were created? God says that unless our hearts are changed, our lives won't be changed. The claim of Christianity and the Bible is that our hearts can be changed—in fact, replaced—with a new, good heart. It begins with believing these core beliefs and personally accepting these truths from the Bible that follow.

1. *God loves us and we have been created to live in relationship with Him.*

This is the most important truth for us from the Bible. We were created for a personal relationship with God! An authentic person is first and foremost in relationship with his creator. God purposefully created you for a *relationship* with Himself—not just to "do" things. Numerous Scriptures point us to this truth. Some of my favorites are from Jesus, speaking to New Testament believers, "Look, I stand at the door (of your heart) and knock. If you hear my voice and open the door, I will come in and we will share a meal together as friends" (Rev 3:20). And in John10:10, "I came that they might have an abundant life."

"There is a God shaped vacuum in the heart of every man which cannot be filled by any created thing, but only by God, the Creator, made known through Jesus" (Blaise Pascal).[63]

2. *God created people for a purpose.*

"You created everything, and it is for your pleasure that they exist and were created" (Rev 4:11).

"So God created man in his own image, in the image of God he created him; male and female he created them. And God blessed them. And God said to them, 'Be fruitful and multiply and fill the earth and subdue it and

have dominion over the fish of the sea… over every living thing'" (Gen 1:27,28).

The Bible is clear—we have been given a purpose both as human beings and as unique individuals. Author Francis Schaeffer states, *"If God exists and we are made in his image we can have real meaning, and we can have real knowledge through what he has communicated to us."*

3. *Failure to live in relationship with God and for our original purpose has resulted in disharmony, discord, inauthenticity and spiritual death.*

"As long as you did what you felt like doing, ignoring God, you didn't have to bother with right thinking or right living, or right anything for that matter. But do you call that a free life? What did you get out of it? Nothing you're proud of now. Where did it get you? A dead end" (Rom 6:20).

People are truly authentic and free when they conform to the truth of who God originally created them to be (pre-fall) and do what He's designed for them to do. First, we were designed to *be* in right relationship with God and to draw our identity from who we are in Him. Second, we're to *do* what God has called us to do: to love Him with all we are and have, and to love our neighbors (family, friends, even enemies) as ourselves. This defines authenticity.

Now, the reality is that we have *all* failed to live for the real purposes for which we were created. In this sense, not just some but every person is an inauthentic, imperfect human being. We live in a broken world. Only Jesus lived a 100% authentic life! Everyone else has failed at some point to live the life for which they were created. God's Word tells us that we were created to be fully alive, fully creative, fully relational human beings, and to be perfect reflections of His image. But then because of the choice to go apart from God, we became dead spiritually and wounded or "unwhole." In essence, our spirits have been deadened. That part of us that was made to relate to God is dead, lifeless. Illusionist Andre Kole uses the illustration of a light bulb that has been turned off in the human heart: Nothing we can do will turn the light on— no good works, good motives or good intentions carry the current to turn the light on of a relationship with Him. "For all have sinned and fallen short of the glory of God" (Rom 3:23).

This is where you and I live, apart from redemption in Christ— we're incomplete, hopeless and broken. Our attempts to remedy the situation ourselves will always leave us in spiritual darkness. We are not able to recover the life we were originally designed for. And as we observed earlier, the remedies we artists often seek only leave us more and more empty. The payback for sin is always death spiritually.

4.   *God wants us to experience redemption and a new heart.*

Apart from the intervention of God's grace, our heart is described as being "dead," "desperately wicked" and destined for eternal separation from God and others. We need a new heart, and this is what God promises in the book of Ezekiel. *"And I will give you a new heart, and a new spirit I will put within you. And I will remove the heart of stone from your flesh and give you a heart of flesh"* (Ez 36:26).

We can receive a new heart from God. If you're living from a heart of stone, it is impossible to live authentically. We are born into this state but God wants to change that...Yes, He is still offering a new heart to each one of us through Christ. He has offered us a way to redemption and restoration, a way to real life and "wholeness."

We need only to believe and accept His provision for our sinfulness and wrong choices;   Jesus is that provision. Jesus offers us redemption. He took our place on the cross and took upon Himself God's judgment for our sinfulness so we could begin a new relationship with

188

Believing in God and Beginning a Relationship

God! He was buried and raised to new life and offers to us not only the benefits of forgiveness at the cross, but also the newness of life by His resurrection, a new spirit and new heart!

We simply need to believe and receive His gift. Jesus Himself claimed, *"I am the way, the truth, the life, no one comes to the Father except through me"* (John 14:6). The New Testament states that though we are born in death, we can be "reborn" to new life through Jesus Christ. *"For the wages of sin is death, but the free gift of God is eternal life through Jesus Christ our Lord"* (Rom 6:23).

The pathway to becoming an authentic, whole person begins with accepting Christ as your personal Lord and Savior. The Bible claims that all who accept Him become alive again and move from spiritual darkness to light, from a dead spirit and heart to a living spirit and a new heart (Ez 36, 2 Cor 5:17). Once we accept Him, He begins the process of transforming us into the person we were originally created to be. We move from a post-fall existence to a "Redeemed-life" existence. The following illustration shows what are the marks of an authentic believer. He/she is not perfect, but is growing more and more into the image of Jesus Christ as he/she chooses to walk with Him and live by the truth.

> **Redeemed-life:** (life in this world having accepted Christ as personal Savior)
>
> - Mortal imperfect body awaiting new
>
> - Imperfect but improving relationships
>
> - Growing harmony with nature and work
>
> - Alive Spiritually
>
> - Rediscovery of purpose and use of our gifts and talents for God's glory
>
> - Abundant life with God
>
> - New heart (good)
>
> - Eternal life with God
>
> - Free will and the power to overcome temptation
>
> - Significance drawn from our relationship with God!

$$\longrightarrow$$

What About You?

Perhaps you've never begun a personal relationship with God, or you don't know where you stand with God. Because of the "good news," the gospel of Jesus, you can begin that relationship right now. By personally accepting what Jesus did on the cross for you and by receiving Him by faith as your personal Savior, you can begin that relationship. It's as simple as that. John 1:12 reminds us, "But as many as received Him, He gave the right to become children of God." Based on this and other Scriptures, if you believe Jesus lived, died for your sins and was raised, and you receive Him into your life, at that moment you will become a child of God.

If you wish to receive Christ right now, you can express your faith now through prayer. Prayer is simply sharing your heart's desires and thoughts with God. Here's a suggested prayer:

"Lord Jesus, I need you. Thank you for dying on the cross for my sins and taking the judgment I deserve. I now receive you as my Lord and Savior and want to live in relationship with you. I invite you to come into my life and make me into the person you want me to be. I receive Your Spirit and the new heart you've promised that I might walk in your light and fulfill your purposes for me. Thank you for loving me!"

If this is your desire and you invite Jesus into your life, you can know for sure that Christ is in your life and He will never leave you based on the promises of His word (Jn 1:12, Heb13:5). Congratulations! You've begun a relationship with God!

Accepting Christ means you have eternal life!

1 John5:12,13 assures us: *"This is the testimony, that God gave us eternal life, and this life is in his Son. Whoever has the Son has life; whoever does not have the Son of God does not have life. I write these things to you who believe in the name of the Son of God that you may know that you have eternal life."*

What an amazing truth! We can *know* that we have eternal life. You received many other significant things too as a result of your trusting Christ and accepting His work on the cross:

- You received forgiveness for all of your sins.
- You were given God's Spirit to live in you.
- He gave you a new heart.

He's given you a new life for you to discover and live from for His glory.

These and many other truths are yours to discover, and I encourage you to connect with other strong Christians or a church where you can learn how to grow in your new relationship! There are also many programs I would be glad to point you to. Please feel free to contact me at: www.goauthentic.org.

What an amazing God we have. I'm excited for the plans God has for you!

Leading Artists

With upright heart he shepherded them and guided them with his skillful hand. (Ps 78:72)

To many, the idea of leading artists sounds like trying to herd cats. Artists can be illogical, spacey, vague and impetuous. Putting a group of artists together seems like it would only multiply the problems. Imagine putting some of your favorite artists in a room, asking them to work together on a project. For instance, say you put Paul McCartney, Stevie Wonder and Prince together to come up with a theme song for AIDS relief. All of these men are very gifted, but to expect them to come up with something good would take more than just putting them in a room. It would take vision casting, strategy, role delegation, encouragement and some executive decision-making. Usually this is called leadership. Leaders often take the form of a director, producer or team leader. Whatever the title, that person must lead effectively to produce a successful group or product. If it's an unpaid volunteer group, this becomes even more difficult and usually requires leadership with greater vision and authenticity.

There's also a difference between being an effective leader and being an authentic leader. Leading a group effectively and authentically takes more love, insight, courage and wisdom. It requires a commitment to more than just producing a good product or program. It requires a commitment to personal integrity, an honorable process, and a commitment to people's growth.

Effective vs. Authentic

Being an effective leader means that you must:

- Clearly and regularly communicate mission, vision, values and strategy.
- Recruit and coalesce others to commit to the vision and your leadership
- Clearly define and effectively assign roles and expectations.
- Evaluate performance regularly and ensure a standard of performance is adhered to.
- Consistently demonstrate your commitment to the vision, values and strategy of your team.

Anyone who has experience in the business world, as well as many other artistic organizations, can attest that this type of leadership often produces good results, especially when monetary remuneration or fame accompanies it. Some leaders are well known for their ability to "get results"—however they get it. In the band and orchestra world, certain directors are well known for getting consistent high-grade results. Some, however, are well-known for their sometimes impersonal, egotistical and intimidating means of doing so. Oftentimes it's the little "communities" that are formed under such "persecution" that provide the real reason the groups continue to flourish. Very often these leaders also discover that treating their team members as "cogs in a wheel" eventually has negative repercussions, and they either learn and change or continue with their egotistical leadership style. I'm sure you can think of examples from your own experience or reading. You only need to look at how short-lived most rock bands are to see that money, ego or fame are not sufficient motivators to keep a group together. There is a better way.

Being an effective and authentic leader means that:

1. A team member's welfare and growth as well as their performance are a concern. In other words, they value people over programs.

Perhaps this is the most obvious difference between an efficient leader and an authentic leader. Don't think that the authentic leader is soft on speaking honestly and pointing out areas that need to change— quite the opposite! But it also means each person in the group is recognized and cared for. It means the leader ensures that individuals are encouraged to give their best and be in the best place for the good of the group and their own growth. In a large group he may set up systems or evaluations to help this process. Or he may simply nurture the ongoing dialogue in relationship. Usually it's good to have both—an evaluation/ accountability structure and an ongoing, spontaneous responsiveness to people.

"Speaking the truth in love" is the goal of all communication. It's important to realize that when you have filled people's "emotional tanks" with positive feedback—affirming their value as people—it is much easier for them to receive constructive criticism. If you only focus on the improvements people need to make and fail to celebrate the progress, pretty soon some of your key players will feel unappreciated and become demotivated. Perhaps you can't be this well connected with everyone, but you can focus on connecting with your key people. You can also delegate some of this care to your key leaders in a large group.

The old adage "People don't care how much you know until they know how much you care"[64] is still true. It says that people are more important than programs. This must be more than just a statement; it must be a lived-out agenda on a leader's calendar. If others perceive that you are genuinely concerned for the whole person, they will be motivated even though they may not get much time with you due to the size of the organization.

Also, an authentic leader's example and willingness to personally sacrifice will motivate people to commit to the vision and values of their group. This only happens as individuals begin to believe their cause is ultimately beneficial to themselves and others, if not immediately then in the future. Perhaps this is why Jesus constantly pointed his disciples to the higher and eternal rewards they would have as they died to their own agendas, i.e. *"He who loses his life for My sake will find it."* In the book of Acts it's clear they had no doubt about Jesus' love and goodness toward them, even in the face of their own death. Amazing!

Note that I'm not saying your organization should be this paragon of perfect love and deep relationships. Every organization will have different levels of care and concern for the individuals in it. A community band, for example, would have different expectations than a church worship team. But, it is also important to recognize and communicate what level of relationships are expected or aimed for as an organization. This way everyone knows what he or she should be aspiring to. Do you have a plan or system to help communicate and foster these types of caring relationships? What do you do to help your team members grow? You could go as far as to provide mentoring or individual goal setting, bring in guests to share their stories, etc. Is valuing people over programs really a value? How is it expressed?

As an authentic leader, the principle of loving others is part of your calling and it should be lived out with those closest to you.

2. The process is as important as the product and it is regularly evaluated (i.e., attitudes, relational harmony, group culture)

Leading Artists

Process is the everyday work that shows our humanity. To assume that our process needs no improvement or doesn't fall short of excellence is naïve because we all have relational and process shortcomings. Everyone usually knows this, but sometimes we fail to apply this idea to the unique challenge of being authentic leaders. We learn from our education, training and experience that there are more effective ways to rehearse or draw, paint, or hone our craft, etc. But we easily can forget to learn better attitudes and motivations, or fail to learn how to more effectively live out our stated values. To keep a team highly motivated, with good attitudes and in relational harmony, takes extra sensitivity as a leader. This also calls on a leader to "set the pace" by his own integrity and example and to own the value of having a healthy process.

It is always good to keep the importance of a good process in front of you and your team. Do you know what a successful and authentic process looks like? Do you know how to evaluate it? Does your team?

Here are some ways to develop a good leadership process:

- Clearly state mission and values.
- Cast vision regularly.
- Develop and hone your strategy
- Re-envision, remember mission, communicate strategy—all ongoing.
- Accomplish tasks.
- Celebrate team and individual accomplishments.
- Repeat this process for the next season.

3. The leader's authenticity is a top priority

An authentic leader is in touch with her calling. Authentic leaders understand that their primary audience is God in all things. Whether it's behind the scenes or in performance, on time or off time, she understands success is defined by having "integrity of heart" as well as "skillful hands," and she prioritizes personal authenticity (Ps 78:72).

In Old Testament terms, the leader often was a chief warrior on the battlefront. As such he was commanded by God to "be strong and courageous." This was Joshua's commission as he led Israel into the Promised Land. Numerous times he and all of Israel were commanded to be strong and courageous as they embarked on the land God had promised them. God could have told Joshua many things as he took over leadership from Moses, but "strong and courageous" were his top admonitions. Modern day leaders need the same admonition. Here are some thoughts about being strong and courageous.

So how do we become strong?

Being strong is a fruit of discipline. Just as a weightlifter develops strength through disciplined workouts, so we must engage in regular disciplines to become strong people with integrity of heart. Developing and maintaining your spiritual life is foundational to authenticity.

Some of the disciplines that help us grow spiritually are prayer, scripture meditation, solitude, fellowship and service—in short, obedience. It is important to take time regularly to evaluate what disciplines you need to practice to become stronger. Proverbs 24 reminds us: *"A wise man is full of strength, and a man of knowledge enhances his might, for by wise guidance you can wage your war..."* It is worth noting that life is not stagnant and we're in a battle whether we like it or not! We are either moving forward or slipping backward. This is why the apostle Paul constantly admonishes his friends to "be strong in the Lord" and to "fight the fight of faith."

Next to our spiritual life, we must also consider our lives emotionally, physically and relationally and ask what disciplines we can employ to develop strength. Do you know what rejuvenates you emotionally? Mentally? Relationally? Physically? Too often leaders neglect the disciplines necessary to maintain strength. Then when they are in battle or an enemy temptation arises, they lack the strength to fight for their authenticity. Strength is also gained when you're in community with others. There is not a place for "solo believers" in God's plan. Again, this is part of why we are placed in the body of Christ—we provide strength and gain strength from being rightly connected! Hebrews chapters 10-12 provide great insight into how to run with passion and strength, not losing heart. Much more could be written on this, but I encourage you to make it your priority to live out Christ's strength in you (Phil 4:13). Make it your passion to be strong in Christ. *"Watch over your heart with all diligence, for from it flow the springs of life!"* (Pro 4:23).

How do we become courageous?

Whereas strength is largely a result of discipline, courage is chiefly a choice of the will. Don't forget that all of this is a result of God's grace being poured out on your life! Courage means stepping out by faith, trusting that God's grace will meet you at your point of need. It means moving forward in obedience to God, saying no to the fear that would paralyze you and trusting in the ultimate victory God has promised. We can insist that we will only step out on a venture when we are certain all our needs and wants will be met, but that is not how life works. God doesn't give us grace or power ahead of time. He gives it as we need it.

Unlike making sure you have enough gas in your car for a long trip before you start, God gives us grace for each circumstance in life as it arises. Being confident of His future provision enables us to step into the water. If you know that victory is assured through the battle, is there any reason to retreat? The real question then becomes, Do you want it? Victory may not come easily and there may be difficult consequences because of your obedience. But, to not follow God's plan also has consequences. An authentic person seeks and follows God's path for his life. If you are strong in God's strength, you will have power to say no to whatever is holding you back. The most common barrier to courageous obedience is fear—in all of its manifestations. Following the life of Joshua, we see the struggle and ultimate victory God gave him as he heeded God's promise, *"Fear not, for I am with you."*

Strength and courage are non-negotiable for an authentic leader. Not only does this keep a leader's heart on track, but it also helps to keep the team on track. Followers look to their leaders for strength and courage. A leader's example can embolden and encourage those around him to also be strong and courageous!

In this day of pluralism and "political correctness" this may be a controversial subject, especially for the "secular" work environment. Being an authentic leader or artist, however, means that we do not leave our authenticity for only certain times and places but that we let our purpose and calling touch every area of our lives. As an authentic leader, your passion for God's glory may not be stated often, but it should be obvious to anyone observing that "things above" motivate you. There are appropriate times too to bring verbal or obvious attention to God's hand and blessing on our lives and our teams. This takes maturity, wisdom and sometimes courage. Paul reminds us, *"Let your speech always be gracious, seasoned with salt, so that you may know how you ought to answer each person"* (Col 4:6).

Effective and authentic leadership will produce a far greater experience for your team and a more powerful "product." It also makes life more complicated! As much as we might like to treat people as simply "part of the machinery" for efficiency's sake, to do so is inauthentic and it destroys relationships. (See appendix: Authentic ministry.)

Leading Artists

About leading creative types

Musicians, painters, graphic artists, dancers, singers...the list could go on. Are there unique traits to these "creative types"? For centuries, artists have been recognized as unique people—sometimes applauded, sometimes booed. Are they all the same? Do they all have the same temperament? Should they all be treated the same? The answer is no. It is wrong to stereotype artists with blanket statements such as "artists are always out of touch" or "artists aren't stable people." Each artist is unique in her gifting, personality and experience. What may be an issue for one artist may not be for another.

There are, however, at least two areas of which we must be keenly aware when leading artists—their maturity issues and their artistic wiring.

Maturity Issues

Maturity deals with issues relating to character and growth as an authentic person. The fact is that, as a leader, you will deal with these issues no matter what group you try to lead. Dealing with these issues in a healthy, constructive way will probably be the greatest test of your authenticity as a leader. It takes much energy and courage to help people "grow up." Isn't it also true that we never stop growing? So if you're thinking you'll never face "maturity issues" on your team (or with yourself), you're kidding yourself! It's always smart to look at your own growth issues first. *"Take the log out of your own eye, then you will see well enough to deal with the speck in your neighbor's."*

Here are some examples of maturity issues:

Truthfulness – Is there a problem with lying or "half-truth telling"?

Consideration of others – Problems with impatience, selfishness, rudeness?

Self-discipline – Problems with preparation, practice, time management, addictions?

Adherence to team rules – Problems with punctuality, preparation?

Respect for authority - Problems with attitudes toward and submission to leaders?

Personal contentment – Problems being joyful, at peace, satisfied?

Teachability – Problems with the desire to learn and grow from mistakes and others?

Humility – Problems with pride, selfish agendas and self-aggrandizement?

You are probably well aware of these issues and more, especially if you're trying to grow in your own authenticity. Do we ever stop having to deal with maturity issues? No. Is that bad news? No! The truth is that when we look back on our lives, it will be our maturity and relationships that will be most valuable to us. While the world around us often overvalues our "production," in the end it's our conformity to Jesus Christ that matters most. Our maturity is part of God's agenda for us, along with the "good works" He has planned for us to do. One consultant says, "Organizations are tools that God uses to help us grow up in Christ."[65] I would add that it is those who remain teachable who really grow. Regardless of how hard it may be to be in or lead your group, it's essential that you pursue His agenda for your growth in it all. When we fail to learn and grow from our past failures, we bring those issues with us into our next group of relationships. So let the growing begin! If possible, have resources available to help your team members grow and encourage them to attend events that will instruct and inspire them. Above all, be open and enthusiastic about your own growth. It will be contagious!

Artistic Wiring

Every person is wired uniquely, with unique gifts. I've known some excellent artists and musicians who are also excellent businessmen, doctors and CPAs. I've also known some artists who you would not want to keep a record of your CD sales! There are extremes on both ends and even if they are very mature people, still their wiring makes them stronger in certain areas than others. So what is it about those artsy type people that might drive you crazy? Following are some personality tendencies you may deal with that present an added challenge. These are not universal traits but just tendencies that are common to many artists.

Some tendencies that you should be aware of when leading artists:

Scientists and theorists have told us that the left and right sides of the brain operate differently.

Left Brain	Right Brain
Logical	Random
Sequential	Intuitive
Rational	Holistic
Analytical	Synthesizing
Objective	Subjective
Looks at parts	Looks at whole

Most people have a distinct leaning toward one hemisphere over the other. Some, however, are more whole-brained and equally adept in either mode. The artistic types are generally known to be right-brain. Right-brainers focus on aesthetics, feeling and creativity. Left-brain scholastic types, on the other hand, focus more on logical thinking, analysis and accuracy. In terms of leadership it would seem easier to lead a left-brained person than right, especially if you are the left-brain type. Random, subjective, intuitive people may sound dangerous! But any good leader knows he needs the "out of the box" right-brain thinkers to spur his own thinking and bring energy to his team as much as he needs the logical, analytical, objective left-brain people. Clearly you need and should highly value both types on your team.

Artists are typically right-brained people, but not all; some move quite freely between right- and left-brain modes. The question is, How can you develop and employ these gifts in ways that build up your team and accomplish your goals? As a leader, this takes insight, strategy, humility and willingness to learn.

Keys to maximizing an artist's contribution
Value and make space for the creative types

When people are engaging their creativity (right side of their brain), they are most likely suspending or ignoring their logical, rational side. You must understand and value this in people if you want them to be part of your group. Otherwise they will either move on to another group or just go solo. The first step to valuing people is to recognize them!

How do you recognize these right-brain thinkers? Do you encourage them to contribute to your team? This can take many forms from asking them to contribute to giving them a big responsibility. You can also use them in areas other than the artistic (music, art, graphic, etc.). Perhaps they could contribute greatly to your methods of rehearsal, brainstorming, marketing, or other areas.

Second, do you *make space* in your process for artists to creatively contribute, either on a team or as individuals? If you don't have a good process, chances are your artists won't feel very highly valued by you. A lot of confusion and hurt can be avoided if your team knows you want or don't want creative contributions, and when and how they are to give it.

Manage the creative process

In a team setting such as a brainstorming session or collaborative project, it is important to communicate that team members may have to give up ownership of their ideas when they submit them. We all tend to take it personally when our ideas or creative works are accepted or rejected. And chances are that once submitted to the team, an idea will at least go through some alteration. If an artist is so attached to her idea or work that she feels personally threatened by a change to it, problems will occur. This touches on the artist's maturity and is often a great growth opportunity. A leader's regular and consistent communication about letting go of one's ownership of ideas will go far in helping the creative process run smoothly and be more productive. Above all, clearly communicate expectations and perhaps exceptions you are willing to make as a leader to allow for the greatest impact of your artists and your team. If you are consistent in valuing your artists as people, respecting their gifts, and providing a clear way for them to contribute, chances are they will be highly motivated!

Encourage Relationships and Community

Making a creative contribution requires a certain amount of vulnerability. Generally speaking, people will only be as vulnerable as they feel "safe" to share their ideas. The picture of the lone artist only able to work independently is sometimes true. In most cases, however, I believe the reason artists don't like to work together is because they have never experienced true community. As a leader, it should be your goal to develop community among all of your team members. We function best when we're in relationship; again, this is part of being authentic.

The Authentic Musician

While it may feel natural to devote yourself to your creative work and succumb to feelings of separation and alienation, it nevertheless isn't a terrific idea in terms of your overall happiness and health. (Eric Maisel)

Artists also need to fight the common misconception of the Lone Ranger mentality. Of course, there are examples of artists who are extremely reclusive and unconnected who produced incredible works. But if you look more closely into their lives, you may find that those were usually just seasons of seclusion, and not their normal environment. Most of the great composers lived in artistic communities where they felt valued. Though many were not ideal communities and some rather inauthentic, they still provided a place for connection, evaluation and inspiration.

You will do your artists a great service by providing an ongoing environment of encouragement, affirmation and accountability. This will also turn into a magnet for other artists! Once musicians can get past their pride and see the value of having relationships based on acceptance and love and not just their craft or level of proficiency, they open themselves up to an amazing source of motivation and growth, both creatively and personally.

Some ways to help accomplish this:

- Provide group events that focus purely on having fun and getting know one another.
- Have annual retreats where you can delve into the deeper issues of community and authentic relationships.
- Bring in guest artists or teachers who can share their stories and experiences of authentic community (share yours, too).
- Have a weekly or regular time to affirm authenticity, community and for celebrating others' contributions. The list could go on and

on... but I think you get the point—be proactive about building community.

Personal relationship building is also an important aspect of this. A young or immature artist may be very needy when it comes to affirmation and encouragement. I'm not saying you as a leader need to personally provide this relationship, but try to encourage more mature artists to pick up and build into the younger. Your encouragement as the leader can have great impact on younger team members, too. Try to pick up on even the smallest contributions by the new artists and affirm or thank them. Chances are that they will remember your affirmation for the rest of their lives or point to it as a time that was very significant in their growth.

Taking this value seriously also will mean that you exercise conflict resolution and truth telling. Every group experiences conflict sooner or later. Whether it's because of immaturity, miscommunication, or sinful attitudes, words or behavior, how you deal with conflicts personally and as a group will exponentially impact your health as a leader and as a group. Sometimes dealing with conflict takes teaching as well. It always takes courage and love to initiate. And sometimes it may even require help from a "third party" to help sort out the issues. This is never easy and can take time, but the benefits of purposefully and lovingly solving conflicts will impact people far beyond their life in your organization.

It is always interesting to see organizations that have "raised up" artists within their ranks who still serve in the organization after years of involvement. It is often because of the authentic community they experience in their organization that frees them to grow—sometimes to exceed the abilities of their mentors. The same can be said about leadership development. Authenticity, character, and vision are usually caught more than they are taught. So you would be wise to make authentic relationships and community part of your team values. Author Jerry Eisley writes:

If there is to be a Renaissance in the arts by people who believe, artists must not only hunker down individually but also develop their work within intimate community. Solitary artists need stimulation and feedback... For thinking Christians to make a difference in the arts, believers must return to an idea of community where creation is rooted deeply within an oral tradition, shared face-to-face in loving confrontation, critique, and affirmation. What is now needed is a place of acceptance where issues can be wrestled with and integrity can become a product of accountability. --Jerry Eisley, founder of the Washington Arts Group [66]

King David led with integrity of heart and skillful hands. There is no doubt that "skillful hands" are needed to manage and lead anyone. But, perhaps the highly creative types require more attention because they're willing to think outside of the box of our expectations or challenge our assumptions. This is precisely why we need them and should welcome them to our teams. Unless you want a one-dimensional, monophonic, cookie-cutter organization, band or team, your leadership toolbox will need to effectively address the creatives in your group. If you are a creative type, you must learn, sometimes over and over again, to be patient with the structure, rules and confining leadership you may face, and seek to model above all a trustworthy character. As you make positive investments in your leadership, hopefully you will find a greater voice and flexibility for more creativity on your team! Just remember, you are not alone and God wants the "new song" to come out of His people!

Follow-up Questions

Leading Artists

1. As you've had opportunity to lead, how would others describe your leadership? Effective or authentic?

2. Authentic leaders value a healthy process, personal authenticity, and honoring God. How do these flesh out in your leadership?

3. Of the maturity issues listed, which do you struggle with? Which do your team members struggle with? How can you help lead them to maturity in these things?

4. How do you recognize and communicate value to your artists? What can you do to make space for their contribution and development and encourage community so they may flourish more?

The Authentic Musician

Resources to Grow By

Artistic Development

Addicted to Mediocrity - Franky Schaeffer

Art and the Bible; How Should We Then Live - Francis Schaeffer

The Heart of the Artist; Thriving as an Artist in the Church; The Worshiping Artist - Rory Noland

Culture Making – Andy Crouch

Program Development

The Mind Changers – Em Griffin

Finding Common Ground – Tim Downs

Made to Stick - Chip Heath and Dan Heath

Personal Growth

Evidence that Demands a Verdict; More than a Carpenter (Email me if you would like a free copy) - Josh McDowell

Future Grace; Desiring God - John Piper

God: Discover His Character - Bill Bright

Mere Christianity; The Four Loves - C.S. Lewis

The Bible – English Standard Version, New Living Translation, others

The Call - Os Guinness

The Case for Christ, The Case for Faith; The Case for a Creator - Lee Strobel

The Pressure's Off – Larry Crabb (any book by him)

The Search for Significance – Robert McGee

Waking the Dead - John Eldredge

Websites:
- everystudent.com
- str.org (check their links to other sites)

- goauthentic.org
- keynote.org

Vocational Development:

Spiritual Gifts Tests:
- *Discover Your Spiritual Gifts the Network Way* - Bruce Bugbee
- *Discover Your Gifts and Learn How to Use Them* - Alvin J. Vander Griend

Various Profile Tests:
- DISC Test
- Meyers-Briggs Personality Test
- Kolbe Test

Now, Discover Your Stengths - Marcus Buckingham & Donald O. Clifton

Strengths Finder 2.0 - Tom Rath

What Color is Your Parachute - Richard Bolles

Halftime - Bob Buford

"Recognize the Gift - Accept the Gift - Execute the Gift. That's the manifesto that sculptor James Surls wrote on my whiteboard and which I described in my last "muse-letter." James has a remarkable ability to make art. He is also an encourager to many young up-and-coming artists. I've been with him walking around an art colony near Snowmass, Colorado. He's a pied piper. So is Bono, who has used his influence for good to encourage the G8 countries to forgive poor nations some $40 billion in largely uncollectible. Rick Warren is doing much the same. His last e-mail to me came from Rwanda. He was on his way to Davos to encourage corporate titans to help those in poverty-stricken, war-torn African nations." —**James Surls** (Bob Buford – Muse email)

"To write great music, the musician must make his life a great song. ... Ceaseless work, analysis, reflection, writing much, endless self-correction, that is my secret." —**Johann Sebastian Bach: Great Music & Life**

"You build on failure. You use it as a stepping stone. Close the door on the past. You don't try to forget the mistakes, but you don't dwell on it. You don't let it have any of your energy, or any of your time, or any of your space." —**Johnny Cash**

"In the depths of winter, I finally learned that there was in me an invincible summer." —**Albert Camus**

"If you ask me what I came to do in this world, I, an artist, will answer you: I am here to live out loud." —**Emile Zola**

"Nothing is more apt to deceive us than our own judgment of our work. We derive more benefit from having our faults pointed out by our enemies than from hearing the opinions of friends." —**Leonardo da Vinci**

"As a well-spent day brings happy sleep, so a life well spent brings happy death." —**Leonardo da Vinci**

"One can have no smaller or greater mastery than mastery of oneself." —**Leonardo da Vinci**

"If we are privileged to explore our new horizons with other painters through brush, paper and pigment, we are truly blessed." —**Michele Cooper**

"Let each of us dream of a community of artists and work to make that dream a reality." —**Eric Maisel**

"I tell you, the more I think, the more I feel that there is nothing more truly artistic than to love people." —**Vincent Van Gogh**

"I think music in itself is healing. It's an explosive expression of humanity. It's something we are all touched by. No matter what culture we're from, everyone loves music. —**Billy Joel**

"Music . . . can name the unnamable and communicate the unknowable." —**Leonard Bernstein**

Notes:

Introduction:

1 Charles R. Cross, "The Suicide Note," *Heavier Than Heaven: A Biography of Kurt Cobain,* http://elvispelvis.com/suicide.htm

2 Dan Matovina , *Without You: The Tragic Story of Badfinger* (with 72 minute CD) , http://elvispelvis.com/suicide.htm

3 http://arthistory.about.com/cs/namesvv/a/van_gogh.htm

Chapter 2:

4 Bobb Biehl, *Increasing Your Leadership Confidence* (Sisters, OR: Questar Publishers, 1989) p94.

5 http://www.brainyquote.com/quotes/quotes/n/napoleonhi163593.html

6 http://thinkexist.com/quotes/john_c._maxwell/

7 http://www.brainyquote.com/quotes/quotes/p/patriley147935.html

8 http://thinkexist.com/quotes/charles_r._swindoll/

9 Daniel Levitin, *This Is Your Brain on Music (New York: Penguin Group, 2006)* p. 197

10 http://www.brainyquote.com/quotes/authors/d/duke_ellington.html

11 John Maxwell, *Talent is Never Enough* (Nashville: Thomas Nelson, 2007)p.8

12 http://www.brainyquote.com/quotes/authors/c/charlie_parker.html

Chapter 3:

13 Proverbs 4:23 (NAS).

14 *http://www.thefreedictionary.com/heart*

15 John Eldredge, *Waking the Dead* (Nashville: Thomas Nelson, Inc, 2003), Chapter 3.

Chapter 4:

16 Col 1:16 (ESV).

17 Genesis 4:21 (ESV).

18 Deuteronomy 10:8 (ESV).

19 1 Chronicles 15:15,16 (ESV)

20 1Chronicales 16:4-7 (ESV)

21 *Merriam-Webster's Collegiate Dictionary.*(10th ed.). (Springfield, Mass., : Merriam-Webster, c1996, c1993).

22 http://www.soundofgrace.com/piper80/112380m.htm - From a John Piper sermon:" The word "magnify" can be used in two different senses. It can mean: make something appear greater than it is, as with a microscope or a magnifying glass. Or it can mean, make something that may seem small or insignificant appear to be as great as it really is. This is what our great telescopes help us begin to do with the magnificent universe, which once upon a time spilled over from the brim of God's glory. So there are two kinds of magnifying: microscope magnifying and telescope magnifying. The one makes a small thing look bigger than it is. The other makes a big thing begin to look as big as it really is.

When David says, "I will magnify God with thanksgiving," he does not mean: "I will make a small God look bigger than He is. He means: "I will make a big God begin to look as big as He really is." We are not called to be microscopes, but telescopes. Christians are not called to be con-men who magnify their product out of all proportion to reality when they know the competitor's product is far superior. There is nothing and nobody superior to God. And so the calling of those who love God is to make his greatness begin to look as great as it really is. The whole duty of the Christian can be summed up in this: feel, think and act in a way that will make God look as great as He really is. Be a telescope for the world of the infinite starry wealth of the glory of God."

23 Francis Schaeffer, *Art and the Bible* (Downers Grove: InterVarsity Press, 1973) p. 41-47

Notes:

24 2Sam22:1 (ESV)

25 Francis Schaeffer, *Art and the Bible* (Downers Grove: InterVarsity, 1973) p. 36-37

26 Rick Warren, *The Purpose Driven Life* (Grand Rapids: Zondervan, 2002) p.64

27 John Piper, Let The Nations Be Glad (Grand Rapids: Baker, 2003) p.31,32

Chapter 6:

28 http://www.wisdomquotes.com/002856.html

29 http://www.musicwithease.com/bob-dylan-quotes.html

30 National Review, February 24, 1989, p.28

31 David Noebel, *The Marxist Minstrels*, (American Christian College Press, 1974)

32 http://washingtoninst.org/quotables/

33 http://quote.robertgenn.com/getquotes.php?catid=155

34 http://www.artquotes.net/art_quotes/m-artist-quotes.htm

35 http://quote.robertgenn.com/getquotes.php?catid=62

36 http://thinkexist.com/quotation/where_the_spirit_does_not_work_with_the_hand/177811.html

37 Romans 1:16 states, "for I am not ashamed of the gospel, for it is the power of God for salvation to everyone who believes, for the Jew first and also the Greek." (ESV)

38 Robert Jameison,A Commentary, Critical and Explanatory, on the Old and New Testaments (Ann Arbor, U of Mich. Library, 2009) John15:9

39 Eph2;10 (ESV)

Chapter 8:

40 http://www.artquotes.net/masters/vangogh_quotes.htm

41 http://thinkexist.com/quotation/in_everyone-s_life-at_some_time-our_inner_fire/12658.html

42 http://quote.robertgenn.com/getquotes.php?catid=31

43 http://www.brainyquote.com/quotes/authors/g/george_matthew_adams.html

44 http://www.brainyquote.com/quotes/authors/g/george_matthew_adams.html

45 http://www.brainyquote.com/quotes/authors/a/albert_camus.html

46 http://quote.robertgenn.com/getquotes.php?catid=117

47 http://quote.robertgenn.com/auth_search.php?authid=63

48 http://quote.robertgenn.com/auth_search.php?authid=5598

49 http://quote.robertgenn.com/auth_search.php?authid=553

Chapter 9:

50 http://quote.robertgenn.com/getquotes.php?catid=135

51 http://creatingminds.org/quotes/self.htm

52 Dr. Henry Cloud, Dr. John Townsend, *Boundaries* (Grand Rapids: Zondervan,, 1992) p.32,33

Notes:

53 Larry Crabb . The Pressure's Off, (Colorado Springs; WaterBrook Press,2007) p. 221

Chapter 10:

54 Bill Briight, *God - Discover His Attributes* (Orlando: New Life Pub.,1997) p.15

55 Friendship quotes: http://quote.robertgenn.com/getquotes.php? catid=117&numcats=340

56 Francis Schaeffer, Art and the Bible, (Downers Grove: InterVarsity,1973) p.37

57 Bill Hybels, Holy Discontent (Grand Rapids: Zondervan,2002) chapter 3

58 http://www.u2exit.com/

Appendix: Believing in God and Beginning a Relationship:

59 http://www.existence-of-god.com/

60 Josh McDowell, A Ready Defense" (Nashville: Thomas Nelson Pub., 1992)

61 C.S. Lewis, Mere Christianity (New York: McMillan, 1952)

62 http://www.brainyquote.com/quotes/quotes/j/jimihendri195405.html

63 http://thinkexist.com/quotes/blaise_pascal/

Appendix: Leading Artists:

64 John Maxwell quote, http://thinkexist.com/quotation/ people_do_not_care_how_much_you_know_until_they/346868.html

65 Bob Biehl, http://www.quickwisdom.com/

66 http://breakpoint.org/listingarticle.asp?ID=6583